GOING
HOME

RESHAD FEILD is best known as a writer and lecturer. His previous books, including *The Last Barrier* and *The Invisible Way* which comprise the first two parts of this trilogy, reveal his preoccupation with the search in life for spiritual truth. He now lives in Switzerland.

by the same author

The Invisible Way
The Last Barrier
Steps to Freedom
Here to Heal
A Travelling People's Feild Guide
Footprints in the Sand
Breathing Alive
The Alchemy of the Heart
Reason is Powerless in the Expression of Love
The Flute Maker
Spiritual Psychology
The Purpose of Remembering
Rosenblätter

GOING HOME

The Journey of a Travelling Man

RESHAD FEILD

ELEMENT

Shaftesbury, Dorset • Rockport, Massachusetts

Brisbane, Queensland

Text © Reshad Feild 1996

First published in Great Britain in 1996 by
Element Books Limited
Shaftesbury, Dorset SP7 8BP

Published in the USA in 1996 by
Element Books, Inc.
PO Box 830, Rockport, MA 01966

Published in Australia in 1996 by
Element Books Limited for
Jacaranda Wiley Limited
33 Park Road, Milton, Brisbane 4064

Cover photograph by Nick Saxton

Cover design by Liz Trovato

Printed and bound in Great Britain by Hartnolls, Bodmin, Cornwall

British Library Cataloguing in Publication data available

Library of Congress Cataloging in Publication data available

ISBN 1–85230–878–8

Contents

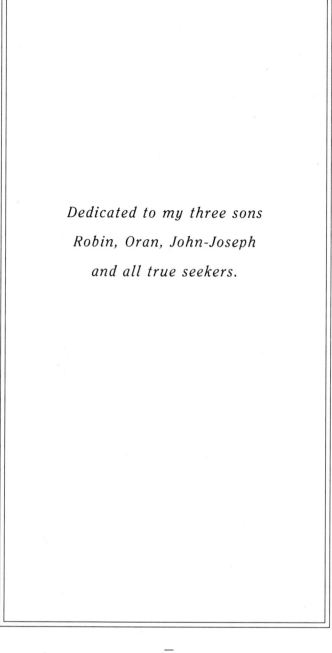

Dedicated to my three sons

Robin, Oran, John-Joseph

and all true seekers.

ACKNOWLEDGEMENTS

I WOULD LIKE to thank my friend and publisher, Michael Mann, for asking me to write this book and my editors, Nick Saxton and Matt Shoemaker, as well as my secretary, Manuela Bergamin, for all their valuable work. I am also very grateful for the kind and encouraging assistance of my wife, Barbara, and my agent, Marion Starck, who helped to complete the final editing.

Also I cannot forget the kindness and patience of all the friends in Switzerland who watched me relive the stories in the book as I wrote them.

RESHAD FEILD

Preface

IN MANY WAYS, life, as we know it, is created from a series of patterns based upon memory. Everything is interconnected. We are connected to our planet earth, and, as the modern physicists tell us, we are even connected to each other in the subtle realms. We are connected to all of the different worlds that exist within the one world of Unity.

I was asked to write a book about what happened to me after my teacher sent me from my home in England to work abroad. I thought it would be appropriate to tell a number of stories, all of which are true, in order to complete a trilogy that began with *The Last Barrier* and *The Invisible Way*. Perhaps these stories illustrate the pattern of one man's journey as he travels on the Road of Truth.

There are hundreds of stories which I remember from my life, so it was difficult to choose which ones to put in this book. I have brought together chapters which are intended to reflect the lessons that I have learned over the years. I write in pictures, hoping to leave the reader with no definite answer, but rather with an eternal question – the very question which makes the blood flow in our veins. After all, there are no answers, only purer questions.

I left England in 1973 and went to work in Canada, the United States and Mexico. It was a long and sometimes arduous journey. I am one of the *travelling people* and I was on the road continuously. I never stayed very long in any one place. I kept moving and passing on the message that there is a way of life which is not dependent upon blaming oneself, others or even blaming life itself.

Eight years ago I returned to Europe. Since that time, I have lived and worked mainly in Switzerland but I continued to travel to Germany, the Netherlands, Austria, Spain and many other countries. Overlooking the lake of Lucerne, there is a house called *Johanneshof,* which means 'John's house' in English. It was originally owned by a Russian duke who was married to a German woman and after they died, the property was abandoned for many years. When I first saw it, it was in a state of neglect and disrepair. I took a huge gamble and that gamble paid off. I decided that my task was to restore the house and grounds to their former beauty, and once this had been done, to hand it back to the Swiss.

This has been a wonderful experiment for all of the people involved. Money was donated to restore the house and many of us gave our time and talents to make this adventure work. Now, the house, the gardens and all of the surrounding land reflect the beauty and harmony that were there at the beginning when the estate was first built. Perhaps my travelling days are over and the time has finally come for me to settle down.

May these stories inspire you, make you laugh, and even make you cry. Always remember that the journey of a thousand miles starts with one step.

RESHAD FEILD
Kastanienbaum, Lucerne

One day walking along the Road of Truth
Glory moved to me and I disappeared
but I kept walking
I walked along a road that was so long
I felt the end would never come
I asked
Why walk this road?
For what purpose do I sing
And walk
And dance
This road of Life?
In one split moment of time
The future came into my heart
Because I'd given up my heart.
To what?
To walk on
Yes, to walk on.
Once upon a time
Beauty came to me
When I was very young.
Don't go and try and find beauty.
Let it enter you.
And then when the time is ripe
You will have something to give.
Why?

Because Love is the movement of Beauty.
Do not misinterpret words.
Let us hear the sound of Beauty in our hearts.

Chapter One

Fire in the Rain

Many years ago, I was invited to build a centre in England. We found a completely derelict farm and restored it to its former beauty in a little over a year. We wanted to dedicate it to the understanding of Universal Love, which is beyond all concepts of religion and beyond all concepts of form.

For the dedication ceremony, I wanted to build a very special structure. I worked with designers and architects who were able to understand my vision. I wanted to create a dome which I once called a 'dervish tent' – a structure which could be taken down almost overnight signifying the wisdom of impermanency. We designed the building so the sides of the dome were like wings which could be lifted up to accommodate as many as a hundred people. However, it had to be supported by nine pillars, nine being the number of completion, yet we had no available wood that was strong enough for a structure nearly fifteen metres tall. So I gathered some friends together and said 'Go and find an oak tree.'

The oak is very important in England, because it represents an aspect of courage and perseverance which is inherent in most of us. They searched everywhere for an oak tree. Three weeks later, in the southern part of England, they found a huge oak which had been in storage for over twenty years. It had been maturing for all this time and it was as if it had been waiting for its rightful place in a sacred design.

My friends brought it back to the farm, and with great love, we cut the nine pieces for the dome. Each piece had nine sides, and the pillars were laid out horizontally in the place where the dome was to be built. Every person who came to the Centre was invited to work on the pillars, cutting, polishing or sandpapering the wood as a form of living meditation. Hundreds of people worked on these pieces of wood before they became part of the dome. Afterwards, we created a beautiful floor with the same intensity and attention. Then we put up the dome.

When we had completed the building, I invited representatives from all the major religions to come to the dedication ceremony. They all came – two rabbis, several Christian priests, Tibetan Buddhists, Druids, a Taoist or two. You name it, they all showed up!

On the day of the ceremony, the weather was what we call 'English weather'. It was pouring down with rain! A Zoroastrian, a young man named Dorias who had been living with us at the Centre, informed me that he had to make a fire out in the open ground! Imagine twenty people with their umbrellas, all stumbling around in a blinding rainstorm, while Dorias rubbed two sticks together trying to make fire in the rain. They did their very best to help him. They all kneeled down under the wall of my private garden and prayed, shielding him with their umbrellas until a fire miraculously appeared.

Dorias then carried his fire into the great dome in a jar filled with dry grass. Over two hundred people were assembled when he lit the candle on our altar to symbolize the Light. We had come together to pray and turn towards the One Source.

At the end of the dedication we were all holding hands and loving the Creator unconditionally, when someone announced that the bus from Scotland had to leave immediately. I asked Dorias to light another candle for the Scottish group, and they took it with them. That candle stayed lit all the way to Edinburgh! The flame was passed from candle to candle and it would not surprise me if it is still burning.

About two years after the ceremony I left this Centre and I've been travelling ever since. I have travelled to many places in the world, carrying the flame of love and the fire of truth wherever I go.

Chapter Two

VANCOUVER

WHEN I LEFT England in 1973, after spending some years with my teacher, many people thought I had been thrown out of the circle. The fact is that I left England with the blessing of my teacher. Although it was not his real name, for the sake of his own privacy I called him Hamid in the first two volumes of the trilogy which started with *The Last Barrier.* Here is what he wrote to me in a letter in September 1973:

Dear Reshad,

To say Goodbye is to say God Be With You – He always is; but this is a reminder that one should be aware of His being with you and so harmonise all your actions with His Wish. In other words, it is a reminder to fide oneself to His Will, so that all personal direction, desire and action is in complete accordance with His plan.

To found a Centre is a part of His plan and if you keep this always in mind, He will make your undertaking easier for you. You have been chosen to do His work for Him; surely this is a great Beneficence bestowed on you. Your part of Gratitude in this case is to see to it that your personal interest is only second to His, that your personal choice is consequent to His, and that your personal impulses are in complete harmony with His – and then easy success and victory is yours. Like all perfect victories should be, it will then be beneficial to Him, to you, and to Vancouver.

Tell the people of Vancouver and Canada, that man, who is the complete image of God, is eternally linked to Him whose image they are in consciousness of this fact, and they were not invented to be a lot of foot-loose and fancy-free robots, unguided, ir-responsible, and left to their guise to be tossed about by waves of a fate brought about as a consequence to their own actions, a consequence the control of which has slipped their hands. Ralph Waldo Emerson says, 'Woe unto him who suffers himself to be betrayed by fate!' But mankind accepts this fate with its ebb and tide as an opportunity for self-satisfaction as a birth right, without any obligation in return. They forget that all right incorporates an obligation. To bring out this inherent obligation in being Man is your job – a difficult job which can only be resolved by a certain Knowledge which inevitably leads to Love. This is the knowledge of oneself. To know oneself is surely to know Him in whose image one is. For the image and the subject of that image to unite is fulfilment; and complete fulfilment is only possible in Love.

Tell them that if they come to you with reserva-tions, with prejudices, with self-centered and self-protective pettiness and bigotry, it is better for them not to come to you, but to find a suitable confined form and dogma which will placate their self-righteousness. Because, our way is just the opposite of this, whereby *we give up the self we have nurtured up to then, for a Universal Truth which is the Matrix of our true self. For those of us who have come on this way with you, we have discovered that ourselves will never again be satisfied, fulfilled, except through that reunion with the Universal Truth. If they want to give themselves up to this joy of realisation, then lead them to come to Him – and this is why 'God Speed' to you and 'Goodbye!' Know that a part of all of us goes with you wherever you go, together with all our prayers for success in your undertaking, and Love which is mutually His and ours. May He in His all enfolding Compassion lend you Grace and ease your task for you and protect you. God be with you.*

I arrived in Canada, having already been instructed to start a group which would study a particular paper my teacher had put together based on the teachings of the great mystic Muhyiddin Ibn al-'Arabi who lived in the thirteenth century. I had never been to Vancouver, and I knew absolutely no one in Canada. Where was I to begin? A young American friend who'd been at the centre I was running in England went on ahead of me. I had asked him to see if he could find a place where we could stay. He met a Canadian man who had already studied certain esoteric teachings and the two of them found a small apartment. In fact, it was very small indeed, and all three of us had to live in it together. I, at least, had a bed, while the other two graciously slept on the floor.

For a few weeks we explored Vancouver and tried to get used to this culture which was so different from England.

We decided to put up some small posters around town, announcing that I would give a talk. Much to my surprise, when I arrived at the large meeting hall it was nearly full. There were lots of blank faces in the crowd and I remember trying to think in Canadian!

I gave my lecture in story form with as much humour as I could muster, and managed to convey to them just what I was sent there to do. Deciding to make things purposely difficult, I announced that in future I would give classes in our tiny apartment at five-thirty every morning for the next three weeks. After this revelation, there was something of a stunned silence. I knew that only the right people would come. Perhaps just six or seven people at the most. Then I picked up my guitar and finished the evening with a song which I often do at these talks to leave my audience in a relaxed state of mind.

On the day of the first class, we got up very early. I had promised a light breakfast at the end of class for those who came. At five-thirty in the morning there was a knock on the door. To my surprise, once again, there were about thirty people standing outside. The majority of them were cheerfully saying, 'Our teacher sent us!'

I became slightly pale at this point, because the apartment was so small. However, having lived with dervishes in the Middle East, I knew that one could make oneself very small if one squashed up and sat on the floor. So I welcomed them in, and indeed, we were all very squashed. I told them a few jokes to lighten up the atmosphere. Then I handed out the paper that my teacher had given me and told them how we would study it.

I informed them no comments would be made and no

explanations would be offered. Each person would simply read one or two sentences and then pass the paper clockwise from person to person. This approach was all very new to them but they seemed to jump right into it. It turned out to be a successful first class followed by croissants and coffee.

After they'd gone, I was talking with my two friends, and I asked them if they had any idea where these people had come from. One of them offered, 'I'm not sure but I know they had to get up at two o'clock this morning to get here on time.'

At the end of the next class I asked one of the women where she and her friends had come from.

'Our teacher sent us,' she replied.

I pressed on, 'But where do you come from?'

'We come here from the States, just south of Seattle,' she answered.

'And how long is the drive?' I asked.

'About three hours,' she replied.

'Good heavens!' I said, 'What an astonishing task! Now that's what I call will and perseverance!'

I was truly astounded. I wondered to myself, 'Are all Americans so highly motivated?'

One morning, a woman in the group said, 'Our teacher wants to see you. He is very ill.' Naturally, I'm willing to drop everything if there's a chance to help anybody, so I asked where he lived. 'He's in California,' she replied.

We had just completed the study course in Vancouver and so I flew to California at once to see if I could help this enigmatic man who called himself E.J. His home was situated a long way from the ocean and up in the mountains. When I arrived, I was welcomed by some of the people who were living in his house. They very kindly offered me tea, as I waited to be taken to his sickbed. Suddenly E.J. appeared in the room and immediately burst into laughter! This annoyed me immensely, since I had just travelled a thousand miles because I thought he was ill.

He said, 'Reshad, I knew I had to get you here somehow.'

I complained, 'But I thought you were desperately ill.'

He answered slyly, 'Yes, that's what I said, but that doesn't mean it's true, does it?'

This is how I met E.J. The story of our relationship is a book in itself. He is one of the most remarkable people I have ever met and it was through him that the next step of the journey began to unfold.

Chapter Three

DON'T EVER GO HOME

WHEN I WAS invited by the East-West Center in Los Angeles to give a talk, I asked E.J. to help me out. He flatly refused.

'E.J.,' I insisted, 'Why don't we do a double act?'

'No way, Reshad,' he replied.

'Look, I'm only going to speak for about forty minutes. Please come after that.' He did not reply.

When I arrived at the auditorium, there were so many people in the hall I could scarcely reach the stage. I don't like giving public talks. I felt very humble. Previously, I had meditated on what I should say that evening and the words that came to me were, 'Don't ever go home.' Thus, I based the whole discourse on the idea that we have to move from our concepts towards something else which is our real potential.

I got on the stage and faced all these people who were staring up at me as if I was some sort of a guru or a saviour. I reminded myself that I was only going to speak for forty minutes and that I had to fit every single thing I wanted to say into this amount of time. Twenty-two minutes later I was talking to a turned-on audience – an audience that was plugged in. We were all connected together.

Then, out of nowhere, five Franciscan nuns walked into the auditorium. I knew the robes were Franciscan because of their colour. But my intuition told me that these women weren't nuns! Everybody offered them seats. They refused to sit and walked down the aisle, marching right up to the stage. Then they stopped, and just stood there staring at me. I broke out in a sweat and I sensed that something completely outside my control was about to happen. One of the nuns who was standing right in front of me lifted up her skirt and smiled. Under her brown and white robes she had concealed a portable tape recorder. 'Oh God!' I thought, 'What's going on here?' Then it hit me! I realized that two of the nuns were my own pupils. I had to continue!

The audience wasn't able to see the sister who'd flashed me and they seemed to be very impressed that five Franciscan nuns were standing before me with such respect. I noticed the other three girls were E.J.'s pupils. The hall was packed with people of all ages, from various backgrounds.

All of a sudden, twelve novices of the Order came walking in from my left. They were all dressed in white. By this time, the audience was completely overwhelmed. There were now five Fransciscan nuns lined up opposite me on one wall and twelve white-robed novices on the other wall. All of them refused to take a seat. They were all my pupils! 'My God! Liz, that's you! Marguerite, that's you!'

Having regained my composure and continuing on with the talk, a further shock ensued. Appearing from the back of the audience, followed by a young boy waving an incense burner, came what was obviously meant to be the Red Cardinal from the Vatican. He was dressed in scarlet with an enormous amethyst on his forefinger. He moved up to the front, gave me a blessing and remained directly in front of me. You can imagine what the audience was feeling by this time!

I had timed myself to complete the talk in exactly forty minutes. At the end of it, I said, 'Thank you all very much. The evening is now over and it's time to go home.'

As soon as the words were out of my mouth, the fire exit door banged open and a madman rushed on stage screaming, 'Aaaahhh!!!' It was E.J. His head was shaved and he was wearing green robes. He stopped in the middle of the stage and shouted, 'Don't ever go home!' The audience became absolutely still as E.J. gave his discourse. E.J. and I were together on stage at the end of the evening. The shock was so intense for everyone and the feeling of love was so deep, that I doubt any of us ever recovered.

Don't ever go home . . . What does this really mean? It's very simple. 'Don't ever go home' reminds us that sooner or later, if we really want to understand the purpose of life, we need to give up the reactive patterns which have motivated our lives up until now. Only then can we move on.

Did not Jesus Christ tell his disciples to leave everything? What did he mean? He certainly didn't mean that we should lose respect for our parents, or our brothers and sisters. However, we must have the courage to move on into an unknown world. This is a world which contains not only the world of possibility, but also the world of freedom – freedom from illusion, freedom in knowledge, and freedom for the world to come.

Chapter Four

MEXICO

E.J. AND I set forth a plan to work with a group of people and help them learn how to live in a completely different way – while still appearing to be 'normal'. They would be given a knowledge that would become a benefit to their children and their children's children, which would also provide a very special food for the reciprocal maintenance of the planet.

We always say, 'Knowledge is given and not acquired.' The knowledge given would not only benefit the individuals concerned but would also help the developing consciousness of the human race and the planet as a whole. We call this the Work of Accelerated Transformation. Our plan was to set up groups in Canada, California and then in Mexico.

My teacher had once said that the Work needed to be brought to Canada and Mexico. I asked him why. He looked at me with eyes like deep pools in a flowing river. Then he picked up both his hands and raised his forefingers in the air. He continued to look at me while he moved the two fingers towards one another until the fingertips were touching. He glanced at one finger and said, 'Vancouver'. Then he looked at the other finger and said,

'Mexico'. Then he joined the two fingers together, signifying that the next step would be to join together the two different cultures, in order to help create what we call the invisible matrix.

The work went well in Canada and in California, but it took a long time to get the Mexican venture started. I had a very strong group in Canada, and we'd even acquired some land way out in the country. I had begun to spend a part of my time in Canada and a part of it in Los Angeles where I started a centre called 'The Institute for Conscious Life'.

One of my sons was even born there during a seminar. I gave him the name *Oran,* which in Gaelic means the Song of the Universe. When he was born, we were right in the middle of a class. I told everybody to carry on while I went up to our apartment to help with the birth. Oran came into this world to the sound of certain chants which were very calming for his mother and also encouraging for him. When the baby was washed and wrapped in a soft cotton blanket, I took him downstairs and introduced him to all who were assembled there, everyone happily greeting the newborn child. Then I took him back upstairs to his mother and we continued the seminar. Such is the Work.

Some time later, I went to see E.J. to discuss the situation concerning Mexico. I explained that I didn't know anybody who was ready to sacrifice a portion of his or her life to start this undertaking. Mexico was a country I'd never visited myself and I had no real contacts there. 'What should I do?' I asked.

E.J. replied, 'I have a friend who knows Mexico like

the back of his hand. I'll call him for you. He has a large esoteric school in Berkeley. Maybe he will help.'

The next thing I knew I was invited to come to an event sponsored by E.J., which to my delight he had called 'The Second Council of Nicaea'! Like myself, E.J. has a very peculiar sense of humour. A group of us drove to E.J.'s home in the mountains. As soon as we walked in the door, we were given quite a shock. I had been to his house many times, for many meals, and I knew the house well. But to my surprise, the entrance hall had been transformed into a chapel with a large statue of Saint Francis! There were candles burning brightly on an altar. I found myself thinking, 'Oh dear, something strange is happening. What is E.J. going to do this time?'

There was no sign of him at all. The other guests and I waited in the little chapel, until we were taken upstairs to a room which had been converted into a conference chamber and recording studio. In it, there was a long conference table with microphones placed in front of every seat and name cards telling us where to sit. Then E.J. entered the room and sat down next to me at the head of the long table. It was he who informed us that we were going to have to stay there until the event was over, however long it took.

I was asked to give a short speech. Although it turned out to be a rather long speech, the people listened very carefully as I explained the inner purpose of starting up a centre in Mexico. I also made it very clear to them that we needed unconditional help to make it work. We must have stayed in that rather stuffy room for almost ten hours. We had a break for lunch and when we went downstairs, to our surprise the chapel of Saint Francis no longer existed! It had disappeared into thin air!

E.J.'s friend volunteered his help and invited me to come to Berkeley. He promised to bring together all the people he worked with, so that I could share my vision with them and tell them of our needs. After that, he'd have a better idea of how he could help us.

When we went to Berkeley I spoke before an audience of more than two hundred people. I asked for volunteers. I explained there would be a training programme based on the nature and purpose of the Work with which I was involved. This training would focus on the art and science of breath and on other spiritual practices. Everyone would definitely be prepared for whatever was to come, even the unexpected. I told them it would require a great commitment, and even though there was no fee for the teaching, all of them were asked to provide their own living expenses over the full forty days of the training. I then told them the training would start on a certain date in January, and I gave them the address of where to go, if they had the courage. I imagined that only a few people from this large group would show up. For there are always many people who are willing to come to a talk, if they think they'll get something out of it for themselves, but there are few who will come to something which would require work on themselves and the courage to face real change rather than the appearance of change.

The house we had found for the training was way up in the mountains, and much to everyone's amazement about forty people came. It was immediately evident that the house was much too small for this number of students. On top of this there was the biggest snowstorm in fifty years that very night and no one could get off the mountain. Everyone had to take turns sleeping on the bunk beds and on the floor. Some slept at night, some in the daytime. There was only one bathroom, but the training began, on schedule. E.J. had positioned a large machine gun on top of the house and in the following days several people just left as fast as they could plough their way through the snow. Still, many stayed. Too many, but the training carried on. The people just had to cope with the crowded space.

While the snow was melting, the next part of their education began. This portion of the training was actually going to assist in starting the centres in Mexico and in Canada. Naturally, to most of the students it seemed more glamorous to be in Tepoztlan, Mexico, than to work in Vancouver where it rains most of the time. The basic question was, 'Who was going to go where?'

I was called away to England on some urgent business, so I left one of my close students to look after the other people and help in whatever way he could. E.J. remained and directed most of the course. He assembled everyone and announced that because they obviously didn't have enough space to continue the training, seven people would have to leave. He said, 'I'll give you until tomorrow morning. Then you have to tell me the names of the seven volunteers who have consented to go.'

It was perfectly true that the place was far too small, and that, if seven people left, it would be possible to complete the training. That night, everyone stayed up late. They'd all been given a taste of the Work and they had some understanding of what it might mean to serve humanity and the whole planet in an unselfish way. They were eager to do whatever they could to help. Some of the people suggested they draw straws, and those who drew the shortest ones would have to leave. This idea was turned down and I was later told that they agreed to be silent for a while so everybody could make his or her own decision. Finally, seven people did volunteer to leave and, in the morning, they went to my friend and gave him their names.

Then E.J. came down to the living room. He looked at the volunteers, smiled, and said, 'Guess what, folks? You are the magnificent seven. Because you were humble, you are the ones who have been chosen to go to Mexico and start the Work there.'

Can you imagine the shock on everybody's face? Now, seven completely different people had to volunteer to leave the house. Of course, E.J. had chosen the most unselfish people to go to Mexico. They were among the ones who finished the training and, afterwards, they left for Tepoztlan. It would take a whole book to explain what the training was about, but it surely has been remembered in love by all those who came. I know it helped to change their lives.

In Mexico, the magnificent seven learned Spanish and continued on with their practices. After a few months, one of them went to Mexico City and telephoned me in England.

I said, 'Why have you taken so long to call me?'

The woman, who was English, replied, 'Reshad, we've been completely lost. We've had no instructions, we've heard from absolutely no one, and we are fed up!'

I replied, 'I just asked you a question, Liz. Why didn't you call me before?'

There was a rather grumpy sound at the other end of the line, and I said, 'Liz, if you don't ask a question, how can you expect an answer? I will fly out tomorrow on the first plane. Please meet me in Mexico City.'

So, this is how the centre in Mexico began and it has continued to this day in one form or another.

Chapter Five

THE FOOD OF IMPRESSIONS

So MANY OF US nearly starve to death because of the lack of impressions in our lives. Yet, our spiritual being needs to grow, and in order for it to grow we need three foods: the food we eat – which is dependent upon what is in it, the quality of its preparation and the way we eat it – the air we breathe, and the impressions we receive. We are responsible for feeding our body healthy food, for consciously breathing a higher quality of air and for receiving needed impressions.

We get up in the morning, kiss the children, the wife, go to work, come back, go to bed, get up in the morning, and do it all over again. Most of us have the same impressions day after day. Maybe, on the weekends, we will go out if the weather is good; and perhaps, at a certain time of the year, we'll go on holiday. In fact, it's entirely possible to survive this way.

However if we are able to do what I call 'reversing space', then we can get sufficient impressions to serve that part of our being which is really longing to be fed by this particular kind of food. By reversing space I simply mean that instead of looking at everything, whether it's the trees, the sky, or the people walking by, we instead open our hearts and allow ourselves to be seen. Even a tree will respond when we practise this simple exercise. It is essential for us to do this in order that we may have enough food to tap the creative force itself, and bring it through the world of ideas and archetypal forms into a world of pure creative energy.

Then we are no more living in a pattern of repetition, based on our own conditional minds, but rather we are able to come into what is called the world of creative imagination. This is a truly creative world, and impressions are vital in order to provide a vehicle to travel through time and space. This vehicle is made out of 'substance' which is gained, at least in part, from the food of impressions.

Chapter Six

THE COOK FROM AFGHANISTAN

WE MUST BE careful about what we ask for. If we ask at the right time, in the right place, and with the right attitude, we may indeed get what we've asked for. People often complain because they don't get what they feel is their rightful due, having prayed very hard for something they want. The reasons for unanswered prayers are many, but certainly one is that nothing happens until the time is right. Also, the need has to be genuine and from the heart, rather than an intellectual concept of need or a selfish desire. Sometimes when we ask from a selfish desire, we get what we want, but rather than it turning out well for us, it reverses itself and we end up worse than before.

Learning how to ask a proper question in life is one of the most significant teachings we can be given. In the Native American tradition, for example, the asking of a question is highly important. Before they ask a real question, they will often purify themselves in a sweat lodge and possibly go alone up a mountain on a vision quest. They make themselves pure and their question clear, so that the question may go on the wind, in purity, to Great Spirit. They will often pray for a true vision or a manifesting sign, which will show them the right direction in their life. This answer, or this vision, is not only for themselves but for the whole community or for a greater purpose.

While in Los Angeles, during the time of the Institute for Conscious Life, we rented a very large house for a residential course. The course was set to last exactly forty days and forty nights, no more and no less. There *is* such a thing as the wisdom of impermanency!

Keeping the intention clearly in mind, I began to arrange a team to help run the course. Finally, we were ready to move into the house and receive students who had come from all over the world. The only real problem we had was in finding a cook! Cooking has to be conscious, and in the Work, it has to be *doubly* conscious. If the cook is angry, then the anger goes into the food. When the cook is loving and conscious, that too, has its effect. I always insist on high quality food. Cooking is a harmonious composition of artistic value, and the beauty of taste is a necessary ingredient in the essential composition.

But how was I going to find a cook who was awake? There was no point in advertising in a newspaper, or in going to an agency, because they would have no idea of what we were doing or why. They might even get suspicious and that would cause trouble. I telephoned all over the States and could not find anybody who was suitable. I was beginning to get worried because there were only three weeks before the opening date. In desperation I got on my knees and prayed to be informed where the right cook might be found.

Now, it so happened that at exactly the same time, there was a dervish in Afghanistan who had a vision that an Englishman in Los Angeles was looking for a cook. His name was Ali. He managed to find some money and fly all the way to Los Angeles within twenty-four hours of his vision. Sufis are not allowed *not* to take action and the dervishes can often be wild and spontaneous creatures!

Ali arrived in Los Angeles wearing a long blue overcoat and a French beret. He had no other luggage to speak of. For three weeks he walked the streets looking for an Englishman who needed a cook. At night, he slept under bridges with the homeless, comforting them and saying his prayers. He brought an extraordinary amount of light to all the poor people he met. One day, in the front yard of a big private house, he saw a notice board proclaiming 'The First Sufi Church of Christ'. He knocked on the door and was greeted by – guess who? It was E.J. Gold, yet again, who was running an esoteric school in disguise. Every year he would change the name of the school to keep his students awake and on their toes.

Ali said, 'Excuse me Sir, I know this sounds a little strange but do you know an Englishman who is looking for a cook?'

Oddly enough, E.J. was not surprised by this question. He answered, 'Well, I do, actually. Please come in and have some tea.'

Soon afterwards he telephoned me and asked, 'Reshad, do you happen to need an Afghani cook?'

I was a bit perplexed at first and I replied, 'Well, I really don't know.'

E.J. said, 'Good! We'll send him round.'

And so the connection was made. You see, it's only when we know that we don't know that something real can happen. When we think we know something, then nothing can happen.

About an hour later there was a knock on the door. There stood Ali, all the way from Afghanistan. He smiled at me and introduced himself, saying simply, 'I am Ali.' We sat down to have some tea and I asked him how he found me. He told me about his vision. It shook me, because it coincided with the prayer which I had made from my heart and I sensed that a true need was about to be met.

The dervishes love stories and we told each other many of them, sharing anecdotes of all kinds. Finally, we came around to the real purpose of the meeting.

I said, 'Ali, would you like to be our cook?'

'Sir', he replied with dignified humility, 'I would be privileged to be your cook!'

'There is no point in asking if you are a good cook. But tell me the truth. Can you cook anything beside Indian food?' I asked.

He smiled brightly and said, 'Oh yes, at one time I lived in New York and that's where I learned how to cook.'

So, he came and stayed with us in the mansion, living in the basement next to the boiler room. He turned out to be an incredible cook. I don't think he ever went to sleep. When the day's work was done, he would lead the evening prayers and sound meditation, and afterwards, he would put on his long blue coat and his beret and disappear into the night. I found out later that he was helping the homeless people who lived in downtown Los Angeles. But he always came back in time for breakfast.

Chapter Seven

THE HOPIS

ALI STAYED for the whole period of forty days and he became a very great friend to all of us. When the cycle was over, he suddenly turned to me and said,

'I have been asked by the Hopi Indians to bring you to Second Mesa in Arizona.'

I inquired, 'Ali, how do you know about this?'

He replied, 'The Hopis told me.'

I asked, 'But how did you come in contact with them?'

'Reshad', he said, 'We don't need to use a telephone.'

I carried on, 'Do you know why they want to see me?'

He looked right at me and spoke softly, 'Many of the Elders have recently died and much of the knowledge concerning the land has been forgotten. They say you know about these things.'

One of my professions is the art and science of geomancy. In the Chinese language it is known as *Feng-Shui*. This is a profound body of knowledge that requires a long period of training if one is to master it. I am very happy to note that it is finally becoming more well-known outside of China. Geomancy focuses on the relationships between buildings, people and the land in order to create the best possible harmony for both inner and outer work.

After the residential course was completed, Ali and I headed for Arizona. I had never been to the Southwest and the difference between Los Angeles and Arizona was almost overwhelming. The colours of the desert, the enormity of the sky and the awareness of a culture that has existed on the land for over ten thousand years was truly humbling. We checked into a motel near Second Mesa. Ali felt I should remain there while he went on to find the person we were going to see.

He took the car and disappeared for quite a long time. Hours later he came back and said, 'The Elders want to see you now.'

So, off we went to see the Hopis on Second Mesa. When we arrived we were led into a small house with a mud floor and there we were greeted by three old men. Their leader was called David. He was almost completely blind and very, very old. We all sat on the floor and for a while they continued to talk among themselves. I was very uncomfortable but we both waited patiently.

Finally, David turned to us with such tremendous kindness that we immediately recognized the Divine Presence within him. He started slowly explaining that he wasn't able to help the young people understand the sacredness of the land, and that they couldn't just throw things like empty cans off the side of a cliff without causing great chaos. He asked whether my knowledge of geomancy could help them to restore a balance? Would I be willing to make an inspection of the land the following day?

I immediately agreed to be of service to them. Then David brought out a map that was drawn on parchment. With the help of his friends he unrolled it onto the floor and began to point out its meaning. We saw primitive drawings of strangers who came on horseback to the Hopi villages. David told of how they destroyed much of the Hopi culture at that time.

The map showed a way which split up into two roads, one going up and the other going down. Again, there were various designs to signify the meaning. Thomas, one of the Elders, told us the story of how this map was developed and how it was intended to show the young people, through the generations, what had occurred and what might happen in the future, according to the Hopi prophecy.

I was very honoured to have been shown this map. I asked, as carefully as possible, why the road divided in two directions. David explained,

'Over the years the Elders have told us that the world is heading for disaster. This is the dividing point. If the time comes when we have to cut the snow away from the newly planted corn, then humanity will take the road that goes down, the road towards what could only be called a disastrous end. If this never happens, then all of us may travel on the ascending road.'

Suddenly I was gripped by a strange premonition. I realized it was getting colder and colder. The date was 12 May and the Hopis had planted their corn only one week ago. That night, the temperature would go all the way below freezing. After the meeting, I returned to the motel and went to bed and when I woke up in the morning, there was about five inches of snow on the ground! I opened my heart in compassion to feel what the Elders on Second Mesa were feeling. Today, they would be cutting the snow away from the corn.

I went back to Second Mesa. There was an air of

expectancy whispering through the little streets. I could not find David. Thomas came to see me with his son. I didn't feel it was my business to say anything about the prophecy. Besides, we had other work to do. David had given instructions for us to go see the place where all the cans and metal objects had been thrown over the edge of the Mesa. We had a look, and indeed, it was true – I had never seen so much chaos. This certainly was not what I expected from the Hopis. We found metal cans, old pieces of cars, and heaven knows what else! When metal is scattered haphazardly on the land, it causes chaos in the invisible world. Everything was covered in snow, so I couldn't tell how deep the chaos actually was. I strongly advised Thomas to get some people to clear the foot of the Mesa as soon as possible.

Later that day, I had an intuition there was something else they had forgotten. Sometimes people die without having the chance to pass on the knowledge they have been given. I suggested to David that perhaps they had forgotten a very valuable herb which was growing down in the valley. I felt it was very beneficial for certain ailments, including any troubles with the lungs. I asked if they had a four-wheel drive vehicle so we could go deep into the valley to look for it.

The snow had already started to melt when we went down into the flatland below the village. I was standing up through the sunroof of the jeep, trying to spot where this herb might be growing. In my vision I saw it as a plant which had a white bulbous root.

Amazingly enough we actually found this plant and took one piece of it to show David. I asked, 'Do you recognize this?'

He looked at it very carefully. He smelled it, then touched it in a very tender and loving way, and looking up, he said, 'Yes.' He explained that the medicine man who knew all about these things had died before he had the opportunity to pass on this particular piece of knowledge.

I had hardly seen Ali during the days we spent with the Hopis. He had not slept at all, for he was busy sharing with them day and night. Now it was time for us to leave Second Mesa and return to Los Angeles. I went to the village and asked for him. He was at Thomas's house. As usual he came out smiling.

We bade farewell to his friends, I exchanged goodbyes with David and Thomas, and we got in the car and began the drive back to Los Angeles. When we arrived home after the long journey, I asked him what he was going to do next.

He replied, 'I am going to New York, Reshad.'

Because I had become so fond of him I was rather hoping he'd stay with us. I asked, 'When are you going to New York?'

'Now,' he answered.

Then he said goodbye and left.

Chapter Eight

THE ALCHEMIST

DURING THE TIME of the Institute for Conscious Life in Los Angeles, many extraordinary events took place which appeared to reflect what people needed to learn inwardly. Many new people came to visit the Institute. Some were serious about truly learning, some were just a bit curious, and others had their own peculiar reasons. At the open evenings we often had a crowd of over a hundred people. I never understood how they found out about us because we never advertised. We just put out the word from 'up-stairs'. Sometimes the so-called right people would show up and sometimes the so-called wrong people would come.

Over a period of two or three months, I began to notice a particular woman who arrived in a gold Lincoln Continental, a vehicle almost as long as a medium-sized boat! She was always well-dressed, and it seemed she was almost too casual about displaying her wealth. Her name was Sheila and she was always dressed in beautiful clothes, but nearly always wore black and white. With my British humour she reminded me a little bit of a penguin walking on white ice in the Arctic.

She always came alone and would sit in the front row, as close to me as she could, perpetually trying to make eye contact with me. At first, I thought she was one of those attention-seekers, so I simply refused to acknowledge her. Nothing ever happens until the time is right. Yet she was evidently patient. Eventually, the time came when it felt right to speak to her, so I suggested that she could stay for tea after the other guests had left. When I was at last free to talk with her, I asked her why she was coming to the Institute on the open evenings. She replied,

'I was sent here by a man called Mr. Hughes.'

'Is he your teacher?' I asked.

'No,' she said, with hesitation, 'not really.'

I began to cross-examine her a little. 'If he is not your teacher then why are you coming? Tell me, what is your true intention?'

She calmly answered, 'Mr. Hughes asked me to come.'

I countered, 'I know Mr. Hughes asked you to come. But surely this is not a good enough reason to be here every week.'

There was a slight pause and a rattling of tea cups before she said, 'Actually, Mr. Hughes wants to see you. He asked me to come and fetch you.'

'Ah-ha!' I exclaimed.

At that moment, my wife became very pale. What could all this mean? I have always been an adventurer and I tread where angels fear to tread, so I was intrigued by the challenge. Who on earth was this Mr. Hughes? Why didn't the man come to see me himself? His behaviour seemed to be ill-mannered but then very few people do have manners these days. I have always taught that, here on earth, manners are the manifestation of the invisible matrix of God.

I didn't want to answer her directly, so for a while we simply avoided the subject of the meeting. Finally, I suggested that even though I was very busy, I might be able to arrange a free afternoon the following week. I asked my secretary to find a suitable date. Then I invited this woman to call Mr. Hughes for a confirmation.

'No,' she replied, 'he doesn't like to be telephoned.'

I answered back, 'Then you'd best go to him straight away, and phone me back immediately because this date is the only free time I have in the foreseeable future.' She agreed to do this, and after saying farewell, she rolled off into the night in her golden limousine.

She called the following morning. 'Mr. Hughes will meet with you on the day you suggested and I'll come to collect you.'

Now I was in trouble. My wife was frightened because so many people in the United States have guns and anything to do with transformation is perceived as a danger and a possible threat to the Establishment. I had to calm her down, but I was going to see this man one way or the other. When the time came I went off with Sheila. Her car took us out towards Los Angeles airp ort. To be honest, I was a little bit frightened. But when you make a decision in life with both hands, even though you still have fear, you just go for it, and trust that God will provide what you need.

As we drove on we went deeper into a poverty-stricken area of the city. The houses were small and shabby, and the land around them was not very well kept. I knew the people lived there because the housing was cheap. It was very close to the airport and planes were landing every minute or so. Then the huge car slowed down, and we turned into a dirt driveway.

The first thing I saw was a junkyard. It was littered with broken down old cars, rusty engines and spare parts. Again I asked myself why I was going on this particular journey. As we came to the end of the driveway there was a small two-room house. The house was a 'pre-fab', the kind that can be transported on the back of trucks and dropped off anywhere. A man was standing to the left of the door. I could see he was armed to the teeth! He had a gun on his hip, and a rifle in plain sight!

Sheila went ahead of me, leading the way. She knocked on the door and went in. Shortly afterwards I was allowed in too. I always try to be aware of my environment, to be awake to everything and to be awake in love. I took in the feelings and impressions of the room in one sweep from left to right. I saw a man who had absolutely no manners whatsoever. He was sitting right in front of me with his back to the door, chewing tobacco, and spitting it into a bucket. To the left of me there was a window and I could see that the armed gunman was still outside. Glancing to my right, I saw a very small sitting room.

It was obvious to me that Mr. Hughes did not live here. In fact, I later discovered he was immensely rich and that he owned an enormous house in Brentwood, a select area of Los Angeles. In front of his desk was a poster showing all the elements and their patterns. I can still remember looking at his back and the patterns of the elements as though they were just one image.

He spat again. Sheila seemed humble in his presence and very obedient. She sat down on a little bench under the window. I really didn't know what to do. I'm English, relatively normal, and this whole thing seemed to be happening outside of time. What the hell was I doing here?

Why was I having a meeting with this man? Why didn't he turn around and reveal his face to me? My feathers were ruffled. I can *appear* to be very angry even when I don't really feel it. I raised myself up to my full height and coughed loudly. At the very least I needed a chair to sit on and Sheila hadn't offered me one. Mr. Hughes hadn't offered me one, either. So I was left standing all alone in the middle of the room facing a situation which was really quite extraordinary.

I coughed again. This time he turned around and spat a wad of tobacco juice into his bucket, looked me right in the eyes and said,

'So, you are Reshad?'

I replied, 'Yes I am.'

In that moment there was a shock, a pause which I can only call love. Love comes in many ways and love often comes when you least expect it.

He brought me a chair and I sat down. Then he said, 'I hear you are a water diviner.'

'Yes,' I replied, 'I have been one since I was five years old.'

He continued, 'I understand that you're involved with some land in Canada?'

'Yes,' I offered cautiously. 'A group of us bought a piece of land called "Argenta", which means silver. It's about five hundred miles from Vancouver in the mountains out by Kootenay Lake.'

He replied, 'Hmmm. I have the land right next to yours and mine is gold. Yours is silver but you missed the gold.'

How on earth was I going to respond to a statement like this? Here I was, running an Institute for the accelerated transformation of psychological and spiritual development when suddenly, I found myself next to LA airport with a tobacco-chewing mystery man who seemed to be telling me that we had bought an inferior piece of land!

He looked at me very deeply and said, 'Wait here a minute.' Then he walked through the sitting room and disappeared down a staircase that went underneath the house. It turned out that he had a vast laboratory under the junkyard and the cars were only a cover-up. He came back carrying a thick jar, like a marmalade jar, and the glass appeared to contain a large amount of lead. He stared at me while he unscrewed the top. There was a small rock inside. He took the rock out of the jar and put it in his hand. Looking at me very carefully, he finally shook his head and said, 'You are not yet ready for this.'

I was beginning to feel incredibly strange and somewhat dazed. I wondered what was happening to me. What *was* this rock and what was he doing with it? Was it the rock that was making me feel so peculiar? It did not seem to alter *his* level of consciousness at all. He went back down the stairs, taking the rock with him. When he returned, he sat down and said, 'That rock was the most radioactive aspect of Uranium in existence. I can hold it in my hand but you cannot. You're still not ready.'

What he said completely shocked me. Sheila was sitting by the window and the man with the gun was still outside. I wanted to leave this place right away. Mr. Hughes had his eyes closed. He seemed to be very far away.

Then he said softly, 'I want to see you again.' I did not answer him, but I knew I would come back for another visit. Sheila signalled that it was time to go. We left quietly, and we returned to the Institute in her luxurious car.

I led the evening class, and afterwards, I explained to

my wife what had happened that afternoon. Then I tried to sleep, but something was bothering me. Who was this man and what did he know? Was he an alchemist? What *is* alchemy? I had studied this subject for years, working with electro-magnetic fields and high-tech instruments to help people. In my work, I've discovered there is a pattern to all of the elements. I felt that Mr. Hughes knew something about this form of alchemy as well.

Since I had gone into this experience with both hands, it was necessary for me to find out who Mr. Hughes really was. Was he in the CIA? The FBI? Was he a crook? Who was he, and why was I allowed to meet him?

When Sheila came to the next open meeting, I took her aside and said, 'Mr. Hughes has invited me back and I'd like to see him as soon as possible.'

We fixed a date. She returned in her huge car and we drove back to the same strange little house near the airport. This time, everything was slightly different. When we arrived, we entered the building without delay. I was brought a chair immediately and Sheila sat by the window as before. Whatever Mr. Hughes was doing, it was obvious that he was going to show us something. He called the two armed men into the room and said, 'Go ahead, show him.'

One guard stood by the open door, while the other one took two soft leather pouches out of his pocket. He opened them both and poured their contents onto the table until it was almost completely covered with rubies and sapphires, two of the world's most sacred gems! They weren't cut, but they were polished, and they gleamed with such a rare beauty that my heart stood still. I couldn't believe what I was seeing.

Why was Mr. Hughes doing this? Surely he knew I wasn't interested in rubies or sapphires? What was he *really* trying to say to me? The men went back outside. I was attempting to relax, but it was almost impossible. Again, I found myself to be in a state of total perplexity. Nothing made any sense at all.

Here I was facing a huge poster of the elements and trying not to become hypnotized by the piles of rubies and sapphires in front of me. Why was I here? I decided to take action.

For some reason I didn't feel I could talk directly to Mr. Hughes, so I turned to Sheila and asked her, 'What does Mr. Hughes do?'

This naïve question was followed by a pause. I suspect she was asking internal permission from Mr. Hughes to answer the question. Finally, she broke the silence and told the story of Mr. Hughes.

Mr. Hughes's grandfather was an explorer in Brazil. In the middle of the Amazon he had discovered a deserted city which apparently was built around a great pyramid. (Pyramids have been found not only in Egypt – many of them have been discovered in Mexico and South America.) These men searched the pyramid and uncovered a rare crystal hanging in precisely the same place as the King's chamber in the Great Pyramid in Egypt.

They continued to explore the lost city, and eventually, they came upon a map. According to Mr. Hughes, this discovery turned out to be one of the most valuable treasures ever known. The map his grandfather had found contained information describing the location of every gold field in the whole of North America!

Somehow I knew I could trust Mr. Hughes. I trusted him

for only one reason: I loved him. He handed me a glass of water and picked up the telephone. Then he dialled his Wall Street broker and bought several million dollars worth of gold! This transaction put me in a state of shock. Why was he conducting his business in front of me? Perhaps it was a challenge to find a deeper level of courage within me.

I boldly asked, 'Mr. Hughes, where do you bank?'

He looked me straight in the eye and said, 'My bank is in the earth. I find the mines and then I seal them up. They are a legacy for those who will find them in the future.'

This time when I left his presence, I was certainly a bit more humble than before. We drove back to the Institute in silence. In one way, I was completely shattered. I had been caught in the world of attraction and I'd been knocked out by the knowledge of love, by the hand of love. As Mevlana Jelaluddin Rumi, the great Persian poet and mystic of the thirteenth century said, 'Love comes with a knife.'

I later discovered that the name 'The Alchemist' had only been given to Mr. Hughes as a nickname. I never did find out the full ramifications of what he did – I only know that he didn't produce or transform gold, he simply found gold mines and sealed them up!

Certainly it was true to say that I was frightened about money during this period. I was almost completely broke. In my prayers, I asked for help. I didn't receive any money but I did reach another level in the understanding that the Universe provides all we need if we turn straight with the level of honesty necessary to be able to read the signs that are given us through life's experience.

Chapter Nine

WILL

ON THE ROAD of Truth there are twelve stations, as Jesus knew, and there are various harmonic patterns that occur within our personal psychology. We inherit many things through the genes. We live, we walk, we die. We make our will. What happens after that? All the passengers of the family who have been living in a boat of the love of their family start fighting over what is which and which is what!

That is not will. Will is gratefulness for being allowed to be alive. Without gratefulness will means nothing. There is only one Will. And that is the Will of God.

Chapter Ten

A Journey out of Time

SOMETIMES when we feel very alone, we start living in the question. Then the Universe can provide an opening which could be the beginning of a totally new cycle in the unfoldment of our lives.

Whenever I talk in public, I don't communicate from opinion, and therefore, in very sensitive moments, I can sometimes see people in the audience as bodies of light, rather than merely being aware of their physical presence. On one such occasion I was giving a talk to around four hundred people. It was in Los Angeles and my sponsors had advertised the talk very extensively. During the course of my talk I suddenly became aware of spirals of light which were emanating from two of the people in the audience. One was a man, and the other a woman. First of all I noticed the light, and then, almost changing gear, as one would do in a car, I could be aware of the two people, who were sitting on opposite sides of the room, as they would normally appear to be.

After the lecture I moved into the crowd to see if I could find these two people. The man had already disappeared, but the woman was still there. I remember she looked almost stunned as though some sort of deep realization had been given to her. She was well dressed, and had long, blond hair almost to her waist.

As I passed by her I found myself saying, 'If you ever want to come and see me, you may.'

I did not have time to even consider my words. When I am working on this level, I live in a world without memory. It is as though I am existing in an atmosphere of light, flow, movement and beauty. I cannot really control these experiences. They just come to me, sometimes at very unexpected moments. Since there is no memory as we normally experience it, I must sometimes appear very stupid when I cannot recollect these events!

The day after the lecture I had to fly to England. A few days after that I received a telephone call from London airport. A woman's voice said 'Hullo, Reshad. This is Catherine. I've just arrived.'

I didn't have the slightest idea who I was talking to. I spluttered out some sort of a greeting.

She went on, 'You told me in Los Angeles that I could come to see you.'

I still could not remember who she was, or the events that had led up to that moment. Uncertain, and slightly panicked, I blurted out, 'Perhaps it's best if you telephone my teacher to ask if he is able to receive you. You see, I am going away the day after tomorrow.'

As soon as we were off the phone, I pieced together as much as I could of the story and called my teacher. I later found out she was a virtually unknown actress, who lived in Los Angeles.

The next day, my teacher called me back and said, 'I have met with this lady of yours. Now you must take her.'

Alarmed, I replied, 'What do you mean, I must take her? I'm going on retreat for two weeks according to your instructions! And the place is on an island off the south coast of England! I'm supposed to leave tomorrow.'

He replied calmly, 'Take her with you.'

What does one do? I decided to do what I was told to do and invited the lady to come and see me. She arrived soon afterwards in a taxi. I realized she must have thought I was some kind of a guru, for since I had seen her in Los Angeles, she had cut off all her hair! It used to be long, but now it was cut short and rather resembled a brush. What was more, my teacher had given her a special spiritual name which means 'She who is guided.' It was all a little confusing, but I gave her some tea and explained that I had made plans to go on a retreat and that my teacher had suggested she come along.

So the next day we drove to the island in my car, and took the ferry across from the mainland. On the way, we spoke only very little, which is both difficult and unusual for me. I had committed myself to sit in meditation for many hours each day, and my guest apparently knew little or nothing about the subject of breathing and meditation. As she was curious, she offered to sit next to me, and be a witness to whatever would happen, and I must say that she did this with great respect, although perhaps she was sitting just a little too close. Insight meditation is never easy at the best of times!

After spending one week together in silence, Catherine finally spoke and told me how difficult it was for her. 'Reshad, the snake keeps on rising.'

'The what?' I said. But it was true. My desire body was working over-time. My meditations were relatively useless as a result, and I did not dare to guess what her own feelings were. I did my best to ignore everything, and eventually we returned to London.

Earlier, I had been asked to help with a young people's camp in Chamonix in France. It was an international affair and I telephoned the head of the camp and told him about Catherine, asking if I could bring her along with me. He asked how old she was, and when I informed him, he said that she could most certainly not come. 'She is too old. You know how strict I am about this subject, and she is one year over the agreed age.'

Secretly I was rather relieved. I telephoned her at the hotel where she was staying in London, but she was not a woman who could be easily swayed from an intention she had firmly set her mind on.

On the telephone she announced, in no uncertain terms, 'Reshad, I am going to Chamonix.'

The day I had planned to leave she turned up on my doorstep with brand new climbing boots, and a back-pack, stuffed with a sleeping bag and warm clothes. She was ready to climb the highest mountain, with or without practice. I did have a strong suspicion that she had never climbed anything higher than the stairs leading to her apartment in Los Angeles!

I relented. 'All right,' I said, 'We will try. Put your pack in the trunk of the car.' I then went on to tell her that there was one other person who was involved in this journey. 'We are not alone, you know,' I said, possibly with a gleam of triumph in my eyes. 'We are also taking my friend Martin. He will be here very soon. I have sent him off to buy sandwiches for the first part of the journey.' It was not difficult to see that she was now suffering from a very strong sense of disappointment.

Martin was a young American hippie. Like so many others at that time, he had taken many LSD trips, and was

what was then termed 'somewhat spaced out'. I was told
later that he had even carried a tank of nitrous oxide gas
in his car so that he could have a quick snort of laughing
gas whenever he wanted! He was very eccentric in his
own way, but highly intelligent, and my teacher had asked
me to bring both him and Catherine to Istanbul after we
had finished with the camp in Chamonix. So there I was
travelling with a passionate American actress, from whom
I kept a strict distance, and a long-haired hippie with hair
down to his waist.

It was quite a sight really. Catherine with her short
hair, and a brand new back-pack and boots, and Martin
with very little except the inevitable guitar which he liked
to play frequently, even in the car as we drove. We arrived
in Chamonix, the end of the first leg of our journey, at tea-
time. The car had to be parked in the town, and then we
took the cable-car way up the mountain, before climbing
the last part of the journey. An extraordinary group of
young people from all over the world were also wearily
making their way up the mountain to arrive before the
sun went down. Remembering that I had actually been for-
bidden to bring my American guest along because of her
age, I realized it would not be easy to hide a very striking-
looking woman, even if she *did* have short, spiky hair!

After supper, which consisted of brown rice and vegetables since this was meant to be a 'spiritual' camp, the
leader called for someone to do the first wake-up call at
four o'clock in the morning. Guess who volunteered?
None else but Catherine, and through her willingness to
help she was allowed to stay for the duration of the camp,
too old or not.

Nine days later, my work was completed at the camp,

and the three of us continued on our way to Istanbul. Little did I know what would happen on that strange journey. We drove as carefully and consciously as we could, and before too long we entered Yugoslavia – as it was then called. At this point I noticed there was a little bit of tension in the car. I never did like driving long distances, and being thoroughly British, I wanted to be alone more than anything else on earth. But here I was, crammed into this small car with two Americans and a blend of energy that was becoming a bit too sticky for all of us. And we were very tired.

That night we ended up in a tiny inn, way up in the mountains of Yugoslavia. I had read about such things, but this was the first time I had been in a room which had a bed that was big enough for nine people to sleep in! But it was the only room they had. Deciding that discretion is the better part of valour, I put Martin in the middle of the bed, with Catherine on the other side of him. I curled up in a little ball as far away as possible from both of them.

The next day we continued on our journey, but there was an ominous silence in the car. Martin played a few chords on his guitar, but smiles were few and far between. We drove all day long, and at evening time, we were still in Yugoslavia with nowhere to stay. There was a sense of panic in the car, and a definite lack of trust. After all, I was meant to be guiding us through Europe and, at that time, I was not doing very well.

Martin was driving, and I asked him to stop the car. We were climbing up a rather steep slope, and there was a very deep drop on one side of the road, leading to a valley and a river which we could see far below. On several of the sharp turns there were wooden crosses, decorated with plastic flowers. In some cases there were also pieces of crashed cars lying alongside the crosses. It was not a good omen. Presumably the cars had crashed over the top, and fallen down into the valley below over the rocks.

'But where do I stop?' asked Martin.

'Here' I said, pointing to a space, away from the cliff.

There was still no sign of a hotel or an inn, and it was starting to get dark. Now I have been a dowser since I was very young, and sometimes, if a dowser is very clear, it is possible to find almost anything that is really needed. I got out my pendulum, which I always carry in my pocket, and stood on the edge of the road, keeping the question firmly fixed in my heart and mind. We really *did* need somewhere to eat, and to stay the night. I decided to go through the alphabet to see if I could get some indication as to what to do. When I got to the letter 'E' the pendulum moved in a different way. 'Very soon we will find a motel, and the name of the motel will begin with 'E', I said hopefully.

I faced a deep silence. You could see they were thinking Reshad had obviously gone mad again. Martin and the lady were standing in the road looking really very dismal indeed. I smiled, putting every bit of my strength into the smile, hoping that confidence would, once again, be restored. We got back into the car and drove off. The silence in the car was deafening, but as we reached the top of the peak and started to descend, we came upon a motel by the side of the road. It was called 'The E Motel'. . . .

We drove all of the next day, but as evening was drawing in, we found ourselves in a similar situation. The sun was going down over the ocean which was close to the road we were travelling on. Again I asked them to stop the car. We pulled over to the side of the road. I got out, waved my pendulum around once again, holding the question, and then, pointing directly towards the ocean, proclaimed, 'We will find a place to stay out there.'

My companions were completely bewildered this time. All we could see was the ocean stretching out into the distance, and the sun had now gone down. Anyway we searched the area, and after the night before, I sensed there was a little more confidence. Eventually we found a very small dirt track, leading out on a spit of land to what looked like an island. But it was too dark to see clearly. Driving up the track we eventually came to a tiny village, right on the edge of the coast. We could see from there that there was indeed an island, just a few hundred yards away.

I found a man who, happily, spoke a little English and asked him,

'Sir, can you please tell me what is on that island.'

'Once it was a monastery,' he replied, 'but now it is a hotel!'

I think we all breathed out at that moment. Strange as it seemed, we had found a hotel. He also informed us that there was a restaurant there. 'If you sound your car horn a few times, they will row a boat across from the hotel and fetch you,' he said. He seemed so pleased to help us!

We honked our horn several times, and finally a man rowed the hotel boat to where we were waiting, and picked us up. We put as much luggage as we could into the boat and left the rest in the car. We were all in a state of shock, but perhaps there is an inner guide available to us all, if only we can find the right way to ask the question, and if it is truly necessary to receive an answer.

After enjoying our meal and a beautiful bottle of Yugoslavian wine, I turned to the others and said, 'We have been very blessed on this journey so far, and tomorrow at dawn, I want you to get up, wash, and then go to the sacred well which the local church has used for centuries to baptize its people.' We had been reading all about it on the illustrated brochure that the manager had given us when we arrived in the boat. 'When you are ready I will come, and I will bring a small tape recorder. Ask me anything you wish. I will do my best to answer.'

The result of their decision to come became the book which I called *Steps to Freedom*. Every discourse in the book came from that very place on the island near Dubrovnik. They would ask me questions from the deepest level of their hearts, and I would do my best to answer them from the deepest level of my own heart. Once the discourses were completed, it was time to move on. We returned to the mainland, put our things in the car, and drove on.

Then something very significant happened which affected us all very deeply. It was my intention to take both of my guests all the way to Istanbul, but when we reached the city of Dubrovnik, one of the most beautiful cities I have ever seen, I realized that the journey, as far as we had known it at least, was over. It was time for Catherine to return to the States. It was as though a window had been opened up in front of me. I could see that if she took action then, in that moment, a new way would open up for her.

What happened next was all so sudden, and yet it felt so right, and so inevitable. I pulled the car over to the side of the road, and stopped. I looked deeply into her eyes and said,

'You must go back to Los Angeles immediately. If what I have seen is true, then you will become known as one of the greatest actresses in the world within a few years. You have received something that the alchemists call "the Ingredient". It is a rare gift, and it can be put to good use wherever your talents lie.'

She had so wanted to go on to Istanbul to meet with my teacher again, but I knew it was time for her to go back. I drove the car straight to the airport in Dubrovnik. Suddenly, with no warning at all, we found ourselves in the middle of a storm with heavy rain pouring down in all directions. When we arrived at the airport, the rain was so intense that it was coming through the windows and under the doors, and flooding the passenger lounge. Miraculously there was a seat on the very next plane to Los Angeles.

No more words were spoken between us. There was a moment of farewell which we shared. Then we embraced once, and said goodbye. Martin and I watched the plane take off into a wild sky filled with thunder and lightening.

I drove on with Martin to Istanbul, and we stayed with my teacher on a hill overlooking the city. I wanted so much to tell him the full story, but really there were no words to explain what had happened. He listened to me only briefly, saying nothing. In this emptiness that we shared together, the French expression *quand c'est fait, c'est tout fait* echoed deep inside my heart. ('When it's done, it is completely done.')

Two years later I heard that Catherine had won an Oscar at the Hollywood Academy Awards. . . .

Chapter Eleven

FRÉJUS

ONCE, I WAS staying in a house in Hollywood, California and because of my seminars, papers and books I had become rather too well known. There were two couples staying in this house and also one woman who had just been divorced. I have always been very intuitive and one night I suddenly realized I was in imminent danger.

I trust my intuitions and that particular evening I was not certain exactly what the danger was, but I felt it getting closer and closer. I felt the hair on the back of my head was about to stand up! So I took action very quickly.

I thanked my host and hostess and left through the back door of the house. I found out later that just as I was leaving, the ex-husband of the woman who owned the house was coming through the front door. He thought I was somehow involved with his ex-wife, which I was not. He'd been in several psychiatric hospitals and he was extremely dangerous. Because I had followed my intuition and taken action, I managed to avoid what might have been a considerable disaster. I was told that later he was arrested and taken to prison.

That night I went to see a friend of mine who was a homeopathic doctor. I asked if I could spend the night and

I ended up staying for three weeks. He and his wife were students of Mikhael Aivanhov, known as a Master in the 'Great White Brotherhood'. He was originally from Bulgaria, and at that time, he was running a school in France. They suggested that I go and spend some time with him at his Centre in Fréjus.

I meditated very deeply about their suggestion before I felt it was the correct thing for me to do. Then I wrote to ask if I could come and stay with them, and received a letter back stating that I was welcome. They asked me if I spoke any French. My French is poor but I felt it was probably good enough to get by. So, I returned to London, rented a car, and drove over to Fréjus, which is in the south-western part of the country. My initial impression was so deep that I knew destiny, or *kismet,* was leading me, yet again.

Fréjus was a very large estate with many buildings, including one main building where there was a dining room for five hundred people. When I arrived, I was greeted by the man they called *le Maître,* the Master. He was one of the most beautiful men I have ever seen. He was seventy years old when we met. He had a white beard and was impeccably dressed. In fact, I later noticed that he changed his suit three times a day. He also carried a walking stick which was crowned with a large, perfect crystal.

He offered me a private cottage right next to his own house, and he encouraged me to spend as much time with him as I could. After resting up a bit, I went to supper. There were about three hundred people in the dining room, all sitting very quietly with their backs straight. At the far end of the room there was a small stage with a table set for about six people. This was for *le Maître* and his invited guests. Every day, he would entertain different guests so that each person would have an opportunity to be with him and meet on a deeper and more personal level. At the other end of the room I noticed there was an area that looked almost like a recording studio, with video cameras and other kinds of equipment.

I sat down and wondered what to do next. A depth of silence enveloped the room as everyone sat motionless with their eyes closed. Then, I realized every single person in the room was doing the same breathing practice which I'd learned so long ago!

After a short while, a very striking older lady stood up, and everyone gave her their complete respect and attention. She was holding a book in her hand and then I noticed that every single person had a copy of this book in front of him or her. '*Numéro vingt-six*,' she announced. There was a quiet rustling of papers as we turned the pages of the book to find number twenty-six, which was a song written in Bulgarian. She began to conduct us and we followed her without a problem. The sound was inspiring. After three different songs, *le Maître* entered from behind the stage and sat down with some of his guests. We sang one more song.

We ate the meal in silence. It consisted of one small bowl of soup, one very small cube of cheese, one slice of bread and an apple. After finishing this, much to my surprise, I didn't need anything more to eat. I'd never felt so full in my life!

I had a brief talk with *le Maître* before I went to bed and the next day I was woken up at first light. I washed quickly and went outside the cottage, wondering what was going to happen next. Then *le Maître* came and led us all up a steep hill. He pushed himself along with his beautiful walking stick and we followed him in silence. Eventually, we arrived at a place where there was a huge rock. The view from the mountain was simply incredible, even though the sun was not yet up. *Le Maître* sat down in front of us and we gathered around him. The sun was about to rise up over the top of the hills opposite the mountain we had climbed. One of the themes the Master was working on, at that time, was how sound fixes pattern. So the early morning meditation was vitally important for all of us.

As the first rays of the sun burst forth, he invited us to sound a particular prayer, or mantra, which was a homage to God's creation in the rising sun. It was called *Om Surya*. We spent this whole time in prayer. The sun was dazzling and the world seemed to be very still. Then we went back down the mountain.

We went into the main house where we were invited to do some special movements which I had never seen before. They were very beautiful, very balanced and they expressed a certain feminine, receptive quality. After that, we were served breakfast. It was exactly the same meal as dinner, without soup. There was music and chanting, and again, even after eating such a small amount of food, I did not feel hungry in the slightest. After breakfast, everybody went to work on the land or cleaning the houses. The atmosphere of harmony and cooperation was very peaceful.

I stayed at the Centre for three weeks. *Le Maître* asked me if I wanted to live there permanently, but I knew it was not for me. My own path was already mapped out and it was all I could do to follow this course. My stay at Fréjus had been just what I needed at that time and I am forever grateful to have been granted that experience. Our lives can unfold in a truly amazing way. Once we remember that life is a gift and we come to it with both hands, then everything is given to help us. But we have to be awake. In this particular instance, I was given just about everything I needed to come into a correct state of balance, after experiencing a series of dramatic events in Hollywood.

Perhaps, by being sensitive enough to leave the house in Hollywood when I did, and by going with both hands to my friend, I struck the right note and the angels carried me all the way to Fréjus. If one strikes a single note on the piano correctly, one can produce up to twelve harmonics. And I've always said that the harmonics of a well struck note can bring the angels. In fact, Jesus himself once said, 'The twelve danceth on high; dance ye all. Amen.'

Chapter Twelve

THE HIDDEN MONASTERY

ONCE MY TEACHER asked me to look after a young man who came from an old Persian family and was a student at Oxford University.

If you accept a teacher, it is probably because you have been led along the road to the right person. A teacher does not necessarily teach you something that intellectually might help you. A real teacher is someone who is able to help transform your life from a state of being in the unconscious or even animal kingdom, into a place in the heart where you *know* that you know the purpose of life on earth. That is a teacher.

This young man, whose name is Dorias, came to visit me and ended up teaching me an enormous amount about the sacred art of geomancy, about which I have written many books and papers. The knowledge had apparently been handed down through his family.

Then my teacher said, 'It's time for him to go to Iran. I want him to find a sacred monastery which has held the knowledge of certain things for a very, very long time. I believe Dorias can find that place. I know where it is in the north of Iran.'

Dorias was indeed the perfect person for this task. He spoke not only Persian but also classical Persian, and having been raised in a Zoroastrian tradition he was well-placed to re-discover this monastery for the sake of everyone throughout the world.

So Dorias left to go to the north of Iran as instructed by my teacher, and his particular instruction was to find a dervish. A real dervish can be a banker, a business-man, an architect, a housewife. The word 'dervish' means *threshold,* which in the normal sense is something that you have across a door. Normally, we clean our feet before we step over a threshold. Some people think that a dervish is one of these people who spins round and round, or who has lost his presence of mind in his total love of God – whatever he may be, a real dervish does not need a label.

Dorias had heard about dervishes. So he went to Iran to look for a dervish. Have you ever looked for one? You would have to be very ready. Otherwise, you might find what you *think* is one, and that would most certainly *not* be one. He was travelling by bus and somewhere in Iran he stopped in a village, having had an intuition. There was a small town centre and one little restaurant. He walked into the restaurant and explained that he had a great master who was teaching him, who had sent him to find a dervish. He asked the people, 'Is there a dervish in this village?'

There was a long silence and then somebody answered, 'Yes, there is one. He is our friend. We say in our tradition *Hu Döst,* which means "God is the only friend". He has really lost the separation between what we consider to be God and man. He lives very humbly in a small house.' Dorias was shown where the house was.

When he returned I asked him to tell me the whole story of what actually happened that night. He said, 'It is almost impossible to really explain what it is to be in the presence of a man who is not in any sense in separation from what you, in England, call the Divine.'

The next morning Dorias had to move on because my teacher had instructed him to find this monastery in the northern part of Iran. He had talked to the dervish about it and told him of his mission.

The dervish said, 'Ah! I am also going to the next village tomorrow. Perhaps we can meet?'

Dorias then, with good Western manners, invited him to travel on the same bus.

The dervish said, 'No, I will walk.' The distance was about thirty or forty kilometres from where they were.

So, Dorias went to the bus early the next morning. The dervish shook his hand and kissed his cheek and they bade each other goodbye. When he arrived at the next village he found that the dervish had got there first! The dervish did not need a bus.

I never did find out whether he ever found the hidden monastery.

Chapter Thirteen

A Stop on the Road

THERE ARE MANY levels of consciousness and many inter-penetrating aspects of being. Throughout history, mystics have described their experiences of these levels and aspects of being. Some of these experiences were sealed in history as cosmologies and spiritual philosophies. Various symbols have even been sealed on rings and passed down through the generations. Many experiences we have in life, in the outer world, are as signs to a greater reality, or universal truth. These can lead us towards an inner understanding. I had been invited to drive from California to the inland part of Canada, some five hundred miles from Vancouver, to dedicate the land at Argenta which was, at that time, destined to be a sacred spot for every-body to live in – a spiritual community where people could live and work and perhaps leave something real for the coming generations.

My wife and I, and another couple, set forth on this long journey to the middle of British Columbia in our small car. It was a very long journey. The first stop on the road came when I was driving too fast and got caught by the police. I was led to a police station in the middle of somewhere in northern California. Here I made the first mistake. There in front of me was the sheriff. He had on the boots and hat and the boots were on the desk and I was there to pay my fee because I had been driving too fast. I don't mind paying my fee if I go too fast, do you?

On the right hand side of the wall there was a row of revolvers. 'Oh!' I said, 'That's a nice collection.' Well, this is not something you should say to an American police-man in the middle of northern California, who has his feet on the desk. But I was not going to stop! I said, 'What a nice place you have.' That was the second mistake. The other three started to leave, thinking 'What's he going to do *this* time?'

I did manage to pay the bill and get away without much further ado. We got back to the car and continued down the road. The road was composed of good intentions. I had agreed I would be in Canada on a certain date.

When you have intentions, be careful not to judge what comes along on the road, because it might be just what you *need* and not necessarily what you *want*. It was clear that, in spite of our very best intentions, a force I sometimes call 'the diagonal force' or 'hazard' was to play its part on this particular journey to divert us from our destination . . .

So we went on. We stopped for sandwiches in a beau-tiful park. We sat down, took out our sandwiches and sud-denly two bears came into view. I went to offer them a sandwich. This was the third mistake. My friends were ter-rified! I very generously gave my sandwiches to the bears but I had no idea why they had *really* come. It turned out that it was the wrong time of the month for one of the two ladies and the bears were far more interested in her! She said we must leave immediately, and so we gathered our things and ran, the two bears pounding after my friend. We jumped in the car and drove on.

We then got to a place called Plains, Wyoming. We were driving along in a small car, and it was about midnight on the freeway and then suddenly the car broke down on the side of the freeway! I suggested we hitchhike but the others were too frightened to come along. They wanted to lock themselves in the car because you never know *what* is going to happen in the middle of Plains.

I said 'It's about three miles to the next garage – I'll hitchhike back!' So I got out of the car and hitchhiked back to a place which had a petrol station and a cafe. I only had a little bit of money and I didn't quite know what to do. So I went into the cafe and sat at the coffee bar and ordered a coffee. The man on my right had a big cowboy hat and boots and I said 'Hi.'

That was a mistake. Do not talk to anyone in Plains, Wyoming! He took a long-barrel revolver out of his pocket and stuck it straight in front of my coffee and looked at me. No words were spoken. And what's more, the gun was made of brass, which must have originated from the nineteenth century.

I turned to the man who was serving the coffee and I said 'Excuse me, I have three friends three miles up the road in a car and we need somebody to mend the car. Do you have any ideas?'

He said, after a long pause, 'Sure. That man up there might help you.'

So I went out into the dark. It was just after midnight as I looked through the dark to see who this man was. Since he was black, it was hard to see him. So I said, 'Excuse me, are you the man who can help me to mend a car?'

He said, 'Sure man, sure man, that's my job. I'm an engineer. They call me Black Jack.'

I said 'Great! Could you possibly help me?'

I was a little bit confused about his name, but it was also extremely important that I was able to drive on to Canada, and he seemed to be the only person who could help me. I thought maybe later, if there was an opportunity, I would ask him about the meaning of his name.

We walked to his truck. He said 'Whereabouts is it?' referring to my car. I showed him that if you went up the freeway a few miles you would eventually get to it.

He said 'Get in here.' So he put me on top of one of those pick-up trucks with a crane at the back, and we steamed back to the car. My friends were still waiting.

He pulled up the hood of the car, tested everything, pulled, pushed – nothing. The car would not start! There was no engine, there was no electricity, there was nothing.

'Well,' he said, 'You'd better come and stay with me for the night.' There were no hotels for miles.

I said 'What a wonderful idea,' with much Reshad enthusiasm. My friends were not too pleased about this, but what else could they do? We all got into Black Jack's truck and drove about thirty miles into the complete wilderness of Wyoming.

I was still confused about the name he had given me. He said he was called Black Jack. Looking around the car I noticed that there were all sorts of wires put together in a rather haphazard way and a microphone and loudspeaker attached to a strange conglomeration of endless electrical paraphernalia.

Being inquisitive by nature, a characteristic which is

forever getting me into trouble, I turned around to him and said 'Why are you called Black Jack?'

He smiled with one of those great, huge smiles which comes only from a generous heart.

'Well, man, it's like this,' he said, 'there are these truckers. They have to get to a certain place at a certain time. They speed. The police want to catch them. We have radios in each of our cars and trucks. We are a brotherhood. They've named me Black Jack. They call me up and say "Black Jack, Black Jack d'ya hear? Are they coming?" I take my car around the hills where we are now and I see if the police are coming. Then I use my radio and I say "Black Jack, Black Jack." That is my code name. What's my real name?'

When we got to his place there were about fifty broken-down cars in the wilderness, nineteen dogs and a pony which seemed to think it was a dog, and was trying to get into the trailer! Eventually Black Jack went to the door and shouted 'Woman! Get out! We have guests.'

His woman emerged from the trailer. She looked at us sheepishly and asked if we wanted to come in. I couldn't take my eyes off the side of the trailer where there was a row of rifles and guns – I had never seen anything like it in my life. 'What am I here for this time?' I wondered.

The others didn't want to come in, so I just rested until the sun came up – I couldn't sleep with all those guns around me!

The next morning he brought us some coffee and said, 'Well, woman, let's get the car going!' It turned out that the car had no number plates and so she simply painted a fake number plate on the back. We were approximately thirty-five miles away from the nearest road in Plains.

They were very excited about having guests. Black Jack told us the history of Wyoming. 'Isn't this the most beautiful place you've ever seen in your life!' he said.

Finally we got in the car. It had no shock absorbers so it moved a little bit like a boat! And because he was obviously not allowed to drive the car, we had to drive over the mountain. I was enjoying every minute of it.

I was sitting in the front, the other three in the back, terrified, and I was asking questions. Suddenly he said, 'Hey, watch those mustangs run!' There was a whole herd of wild horses. He took a huge revolver out of the glove compartment and, winding down the window on my side of the car, he shot at the horses through the open window!

Somehow we eventually got back to the freeway and drove up to my little car. As Black Jack had not been able to make it start, I said, 'Let me try.' So I got into the car, turned the key and the engine started immediately! Black Jack let out a few four-lettered words and we could not believe it! We tried to offer him some money for his trouble, but he refused to take it. He just shook his head, flashed us one of his enormous smiles and left. So we continued our journey to Canada.

We finally arrived at our destination in time to dedicate the land in Argenta without another stop on the road.

Chapter Fourteen

The World of the Heart

Can you let another human being into your life and into your heart? The truth is not that God is in your heart, but that you are in the Heart of God. The first time I let someone into my heart, I died. I died to ambition. I completely died in so many ways. If we can let someone into our life, into our heart, without fear but with gratefulness, courage and trust, then the true knowledge of Unity is possible.

In the world of the heart
There are ninety shades of green
In the leaves of a tree
In the world of the heart
There are endless touches
Of man and woman
In the world of the heart
Crystals can sing
In the world of the heart
The earth turns to the beauty
That God gave us
In the world of the heart
I sing a song

Chapter Fifteen

THE WEDDING GIFT

WHEN I WAS living in Canada I had rented a small house on the Campbell River in British Colombia. Shortly afterwards, I met two of the kindest people I have ever known. They were married, and the husband worked as a forest ranger and a fishing guide. His wife now works for the Canadian government, helping the Native Americans to maintain their own freedom and dignity.

One day, I received a wedding invitation from two of my students in Vancouver. I didn't know what to give them as a gift, and I had very little money at the time, so I asked my friend George, the fishing guide to take me fishing. 'Whatever I catch, I'll give to them,' I said.

In this particular fishing area you could catch anything from a codfish to a shark, but my aim was to catch a great salmon! One of my great heroes is Ernest Hemingway, who was a fisherman all his life. So George and I went out early in the morning before dawn. It was cool. The first light split the ocean and the sky. There were few boats on the water, mainly professional fishermen. My guide would never do anything to harm the ecology of the water or the land, so we had to catch our own bait! We went to a place called Indian Village. About half a mile from the shoreline there was a flow of water where we knew there would be herring. Our intention was to catch the herring without damaging them, because we planned to use them as bait to catch the salmon. Isn't it true that you always have to catch something in order to catch something else?

George turned off the engine, and the boat drifted under a high cliff. To catch the herring, he used a flexible wooden pole about fourteen feet long with about a hundred needles sticking out from the end. He would plunge it deep into the ocean, quickly pull it out and then shake the herring off the pole into a special box filled with running ocean water.

After gathering the herring we went straight out into rough water. The whole ocean was moving. A huge swell lifted our little boat up and up. We let down the lines. We'd caught the herring and now we were after the salmon. The boat surged round and round in a vortex of wild water.

Within minutes George had a fish on his line. I watched him bring it in with great care and confidence. It was a large cod. Suddenly I felt a strong tug on my fishing line. I had hooked into a giant salmon which towed us first in one direction, then in another! After running for two miles, we finally got the fish into the boat. It was the biggest salmon I'd ever seen!

I'd gone out fishing with only one purpose. To give something unique and wonderful to my friends who were getting married. God is the Only Provider and He knows best. The salmon was so big I didn't know how I was going to bring it all the way to Vancouver. The journey from Campbell River took four and a half hours. George said we could pack it in dry ice and it would keep nicely. I stared at the fish and said,

'But how on earth am I going to cook it?'
He asked me, 'How many people do you have to feed?'
'Sixty-four,' I replied.
'Maybe you'll need to catch another one?' he said.
'No,' I insisted, 'this one will feed everybody.'

We found some people to help wrap the fish in dry ice. They put it in the car, and I drove down to the city at high speed. I reached the ferry in four hours and crossed over to Vancouver. It was a major task to carry the fish into the kitchen. What's more, it was obvious that this salmon was too big to fit into the oven. We had to cut it in half, and find a plate big enough to put it on.

I prepared the salmon for all the people at the wedding, decorated it most beautifully, and served it to the sixty-four guests. However, I was amazed to see that after everyone was full, there was still another half left. One could ask, how was this possible? There were many discussions later because it was technically impossible to feed sixty-four people on a *whole* fish of that size, let alone on *half* of the fish. Perhaps it had something to do with the quality of the intention that went into that day's fishing that added a certain ingredient to the fish, so that people felt content with whatever they were given and did not need more.

Perhaps when you are fishing for Love, and catching Love, and being caught *by* Love, you can feed an enormous amount of people. Did not Jesus Christ do this? 'Where,' as a famous Sheikh once asked, 'is the Jesus of your own being?'

Chapter Sixteen

The Two Sheriffs and the Béarnaise Sauce

I WAS INVITED to Sedona, Arizona, to give some talks and classes on geomancy. The couple who invited me were very fine people. She was a cellist in the symphony and he was a painter, a fine artist who'd originally come from South America.

He had become almost completely blind. He was a very devout Christian, and a meditator too. When he'd lost almost ninety per cent of his sight, he turned to God and said, 'Whatever I have left of my sight I will give to You. I will become a painter.' Until that time he'd never painted in his life, but then he became one of the most famous painters in the Southwest. They had a beautiful home and my wife and I stayed with them for three weeks until we found a place of our own.

At the end of our stay, I wanted very much to give something back to them. Their kindness and hospitality had been truly remarkable. But what could one give to somebody who already has everything? I decided that the best I could do would be to take them out for a really delightful evening. I wanted to give them a night to remember.

I'd heard of a Swiss chef, who had a very expensive

restaurant on the outskirts of Sedona. My artist friend had once been a sauce chef at Maxim's in Chicago. What he did when he was working there was like pure alchemy. Obviously, it was a dangerous move to invite him to a restaurant in Arizona, but since the chef was Swiss, I thought that it should be good.

I reserved a table and made special arrangements to pick them up. I was looking forward to having a great dinner. When we arrived we were greeted by the chef, who was also the owner of the restaurant. There were about thirty people in the dining room. We sat down and began the evening by opening a bottle of the best champagne. Afterwards, we had some more wine and looked at the menu. I was full of my usual enthusiasm, and perhaps I wasn't listening to what was being said at that moment. Instead, I was just longing to give something back 'with a love beyond all measure'.

It didn't take long before I noticed that my guest was not particularly happy. He wore enormously thick pebble glasses and it was hard for me to see what was in his eyes, but since I was sitting close to him I could feel that something was bubbling up in him and it was not indigestion! He had a very Latin temperament and he was definitely not pleased with what was going on. So, to keep things moving, I started telling jokes and he joined in with some stories of his own. But I could sense there was something amiss.

Finally, the main course arrived. He'd ordered a medium steak with béarnaise sauce. I had ordered the same. I do admit that the sauce didn't taste like a béarnaise sauce to me but I was never a sauce chef at Maxim's. Suddenly my friend was glowing bright red! His cheeks were blushing like the topknot of an angry turkey! He glared at me through his thick glasses, stood up and asked to be excused.

Then he picked up his plate with the steak and the béarnaise sauce and loudly demanded to see the chef. The whole restaurant went into a stunned silence. I, being English, was used to such things, but Americans are not. The chef came out of his kitchen and walked timidly over to our table. He was about half the size of my guest who shoved the plate right under his nose, and shouted, 'You think this is a béarnaise sauce? This is not a béarnaise sauce! This is a burnt piece of rubbish!'

I was sitting calmly, not quite knowing what to do. My friend went on shouting at the chef, who seemed to be taking it all in his stride. My guest finally sat down. He was still fuming. His glasses were literally steamed up! His wife didn't know how to react but she was obedient to him and always gave him her support. My wife made no comment. Little by little, all the guests in the restaurant quietly paid their bills and left. In America, you shouldn't complain, and if and when you do, you must be very careful about it. The chef disappeared back into the kitchen. We remained sitting at our table and we started talking about the inner meaning of Sufism and how it's related to Catholicism. I always like to deal with one situation, and move on to another as if nothing had happened. As far as I'm concerned, living in the moment is the only way to live.

Suddenly, one of the most enormous men I've ever seen walked into the restaurant. He was the sheriff of Sedona and he was accompanied by his deputy, a miniature version of himself, both of them wearing the inevitable cowboy hats and boots. They reminded me of Tweedle-Dum and Tweedle-Dee. When they walked in, I was shocked to see them, because I'd forgotten how wild this confrontation had actually been. They looked so funny when they first came into the restaurant that it almost made me laugh. But I controlled myself.

The owner of the restaurant ran into the dining room to join the confrontation. Both of the sheriffs walked over to me and the big one looked me in the eye and said,

'Did you eat your food?'

I replied, 'Yes, hummm, yes I did.'

Then he asked, 'Did you pay for it?'

'Yes, I did', I answered, ' The money is right here on the table with the bill.'

He continued to question me, 'Have you got any complaints about the food?'

At this point, I was starting to get terrified. Was my South American friend going to jump up and shout at the sheriff about the béarnaise sauce? It was quite obvious to me that the sheriff had never heard of the word 'béarnaise', let alone 'sauce'. The sheriff looked so threatening and dangerous that we nearly panicked. Instead, we all started breathing together. Then I pointed again to the money on the table. Of course I had paid the bill and I'd left a suitable tip. It didn't make one bit of difference whether I liked the béarnaise sauce or not.

I stood up, raised myself to my full height, and with a smile in my heart and a straight face, I went right up to the sheriff, stared him down, and said, 'You have three children, don't you?'

The sheriff began to melt like rose ice cream on a hot summer's day.

'How do you know?' he asked softly.

I grinned and replied, 'Because I have three, as well.' Everybody smiled. After this one simple confrontation in love, everything went well. Both the sheriffs were happy when they left and my friend even showed the Swiss chef how to make a real béarnaise sauce.

The next morning when I was getting ready to go over to our new house, my host and hostess gave me a gift – a cowboy hat just like the sheriff's! They had gone to a hat shop earlier in the day and bumped into him on the way. He was dressed in civilian clothes but they recognized him. My friend had asked,

'Aren't you the sheriff from last night?'

They were both amazed.

'Yes, I am,' the sheriff replied.

'Can you tell me the size of your head? I think it might be the same size as my friend with the three sons.'

I still have that cowboy hat to this day.

Chapter Seventeen

FAREWELL, SEDONA

AFTER SIX MONTHS of giving workshops and lectures in Sedona, I felt it was time to move on and was waiting to find out where I was going next. We lived in a big house near a golf course, in a community with six other people, surrounded by spectacular scenery and incredible beauty. Then, out of the blue, my wife and I received an invitation to help with a project in Texas. The people we knew in Sedona had been very kind to me, so I decided to invite them all to a farewell party. On the day of the party, a close friend of mine and his wife arrived from Boulder to help with the packing and accompany us to Texas. He was a scholar and historian and he had never been to this part of the USA before.

I said to him, 'Before the party starts I want to take you to see some petroglyphs.' These petroglyphs are wonderful Native American drawings painted onto rock and hidden in the mountains. So seven of us embarked on the steep climb up the mountain to find them. Unfortunately, I forgot to take water and that day it was extremely hot. We climbed over barbed wire fences and scampered up the rocks with great enthusiasm. Meanwhile, back at the ranch house, my wife was preparing to receive half of Sedona.

We finally reached the petroglyphs and they were so old and beautiful that I was inspired to talk about them with my friends. Time passed. Suddenly, I looked at my watch. It was already late in the afternoon. 'The party!' I exclaimed. I had forgotten about the party and I knew my wife would be furious!

The desert heat had made us all very thirsty and I knew we had to come down the mountain fast. I could see our house at the edge of the golf course. It looked so small from where we were. We certainly needed to hurry and we were heading down the mountain at full speed when I slipped and fell into a large cactus. The pain was over-whelming. All at once I had more than a hundred spiky needles stuck in my backside.

My friends helped me back to the house. Slowly. The others were waiting for us and were extremely concerned because the guests had already started to arrive. We were cooking for about two hundred people and we had left her to prepare everything on her own. I hobbled along looking somewhat like a wounded porcupine. They guided me over to the bed and I lay down on my stomach. The needles, which were over two inches long, had gone right through my trousers and shirt and into my back. I began to realize they were hallucinogenic, and the experience shifted from being painful into being wonderfully bizarre. My wife arrived, grabbed a pair of pliers and began pulling the needles out one by one. This made me very cross.

It seemed to me as though hundreds of strangers were wandering through my bedroom. Apparently I sat up, with the cactus needles still sticking out of my body, and said,

'Who are these people? Why are they here?' My wife asked me what time it was.

'I don't know,' I replied.

She asked me, 'What day is it?'

'I don't know,' I answered 'Who are all these people and where did they come from?' I shouted.

She replied, 'Reshad, this is our farewell party.'

'Oh!' I said to myself. I fell back down on the bed and she removed the rest of the needles. I rested for another fifteen minutes or so. I could hear a friend of mine playing jazz on the piano in the next room. The party was beginning to rock. I got up, put on my best clothes, and joined my guests as if nothing had happened. We danced the night away and the next morning we packed our things and left for Texas.

Chapter Eighteen

PLANTING TREES IN TEXAS

A COUPLE who had attended one of my seminars owned a large portion of land in the Panhandle of Texas. The Panhandle is an enormous area of high, rugged plains, jutting up from the top of the great state of Texas. There aren't many trees in this part of Texas. It is real cowboy country. This couple wanted to plant a large grove of trees, in the belief that this would be a marvellous contribution to the overall picture of the land. They wrote to me and told me of their vision and asked for my 'help'. I told them, 'This is a wonderful idea. The trees will help change the atmosphere, balance the weather, and provide more food and shelter for the birds and other animals. And of course it will add beauty to the land.'

I told them I would get there as soon as I could. I also promised to gather together a work-team to help. News of this project soon spread around to all my friends. A doctor from New England heard about it and donated almost a thousand baby trees, which were quickly shipped to Texas.

A team of some eight dedicated people from all over the States began travelling to Texas. Some came from California, some from Colorado, Arizona, New England,

and some from other parts of Texas. My wife and I got there first, a few days before the others. It was a long journey. We were absolutely amazed by the vast empty space of the land. It is really like a vast plain that stretches out forever.

We were given our friends' family house to stay in, while they moved into a very humble wooden cottage nearby. The house stood alone on the rise of a small hill. From there, the view seemed endless. The property itself was so huge, you couldn't see the end of it! Just before dark, the land turns a deep blue, like the ocean at twilight. I'd never seen so many stars at night. They seemed to blend into the earth. Then, if one lies on one's back and looks upwards, it is almost as if one can see through those stars into dimensions far beyond.

I often talk about being awake to impressions. Our first impression of this place was when we drove along the private driveway, which stretched nearly three miles from the main road. My wife was driving. We were about half way up the driveway when I spotted a pick-up truck with a horse trailer and two horses peering out from the sides. The truck was moving towards us at high speed and as we came closer, I wanted to stop and say hello, since they must have been friends of the couple inviting us. Both vehicles came to a halt at the same time. The driver of the pick-up and the old man accompanying him were both wearing cowboy hats. They say that true cowboys never take off their hats or boots, even in bed. Looking at them, I knew they were real Texas cowboys, just like their fathers and grandfathers.

The driver looked down at me from his large pick-up and said in a Texas drawl,

'So you must be Dr Feild.'

'Yes, I am,' I replied.

'Well,' he drawled, 'we knew y'all were comin'. By the way . . . my name's Rob. What are y'all drinkin'?'

I answered in my best British, 'Actually, I'm having a beer.' I was sipping on a bottle of English Ale.

Rob grinned 'You should be drinkin' some Texas beer. Would you like some?'

He held up a half-full bottle of American whiskey. I don't like whiskey but we all had a sip, just to be polite.

From that moment on, Rob and I became great friends and we spent as much time together as possible. Rob was the guardian of the old man who had been the foreman on the ranch. Rob was the current foreman and he taught me a lot about the mystical side of cowboys and some of the traditional ways of western living that go back generations.

Early in our second evening there, Rob found me looking around the land where we intended to plant the trees. He took me aside and asked, 'Reshad, have ya ever been to a Texas honky-tonk?' I didn't have a clue what a honky-tonk was. But I had a clearer idea when he said, 'Your wife can't come.'

So, Rob and I went off to a Texas honky-tonk. It turned out to be a dance with loud Western country music and a lot of cowboy hats, which could be a preliminary to almost anything. We didn't get into 'almost anything', but we did witness the beautiful side of true Texas hospitality, flow and laughter. Indeed, living in Texas is a completely different way of life from anything else I've ever experienced.

The next day the baby tree saplings arrived and so did

our team of tree-planters. The weather was getting chilly, for it was near the end of autumn. We must have been quite a sight! Locals would come from miles around to watch this odd looking bunch of characters on their knees digging holes and planting trees on the Panhandle of Texas. We even made front-page news in the local newspaper.

We used to stop the traffic early in the morning. There we were, armed with shovels, digging three thousand holes, which I had correctly laid out according to the laws of geomancy. Then, we lined up each tree, one by one, until they were all facing the right direction. When we planted the trees, we filled each one of the holes with special soil from another state. I believe we sang our way through the whole of the tree-planting ceremony, and within a few days, we had planted all three thousand trees. We patted down the earth with our bare hands and watered the trees with as much consciousness as we could. The work was completed and we stood back to have a look, leaning on our spades, feeling quite proud of ourselves. Most of us had bought cowboy hats by that time and some of us even had boots. We looked like something out of those early photographs of the American West, where you see a bunch of old men gathered around, leaning on their shovels. After planting the trees, the most important thing was to water them, and so we gave them lots of water.

Unfortunately, that very night the weather turned cold and the whole Panhandle froze solid. Then a blizzard rolled in from the north! We had returned to the big house for a celebration. Throughout the whole area, the earth and sky turned pure white and you couldn't see anything.

Our trees would possibly have been all right if we

hadn't given them so much water, but when the storm came, all the edges of the holes turned to ice and the three thousand trees died. Not one of them survived.

This may sound like a disaster and, of course, in some ways it was. But certainly, the impressions we received and the ones that we gave will not be forgotten by any of the people who were involved. So many things had happened and every time I remember this part of my life, my heart sings at the beauty of it. It was extremely tough in every way and the work was very hard but there was a positive side to it all: we were total failures, as far as the planting of trees was concerned, but the experience gave birth to many ideas in the hearts and minds of all of us. For instance, the people who owned the property became so interested in trees that they studied to find out if it *was* possible to plant trees in the Texas Panhandle and what sort of trees would be best for that area.

I haven't been to Texas for several years, but the last time I heard from my friends, they *had* successfully planted trees around the house and these trees have grown healthy and strong. Thus, our journey actually did bear fruit, after all.

Chapter Nineteen

THE BLUE HOUSE

AFTER OUR apparent failure with the trees in Texas, the question was 'Where should we go now?' There is a saying that you are not allowed to go anywhere unless you are invited. Doing this would be like knocking on a stranger's door, opening it, and then going into his or her home. We can never learn the meaning of manners without understanding the true nature of permission and invitation. But first of all, it is necessary to be patient, and this is not easy for any of us.

This time I didn't have to wait very long. Some people I knew in northern California, who had been students of mine, asked me to come back to northern California, to found a school and run a community house. So, off we drove back to California.

We found an appropriate house right away. Since it was blue, we called it the 'Blue House'. When we took on the lease, we didn't know that it had actually been a sanctuary for dope dealers, who used it when passing through the area. The house had a most peculiar atmosphere so we got to work cleaning and washing the walls and ceilings with rosewater, as a form of purification. The garden was a wreck. There were odd pieces of metal lying around, portions of old cars and all sorts of ungodly-looking objects – all of which had to be cleared out. We rented the necessary equipment for the upkeep of the house and then we moved in.

We had not been living there for more than thirty-six hours when there was a knock on the door. I went to the upstairs window, glanced down, and saw a very shaggy, rough-looking young man. He had the dirtiest hair I have ever seen. He was carrying a very small backpack. I went downstairs, opened the door, and immediately was overwhelmed by such a feeling of compassion! He looked so lost and lonely that I wanted only to invite him in and comfort him. However, I was a little wary of him, so I simply asked, 'How can I help you?'

He replied, 'Can I stay with you for a while?'

I looked at him carefully and realized he was suffering from acute malnutrition. He looked as if he'd been on the road with nothing to eat for days. I said, 'Can you tell me why you're here and how you came to know this house?'

'Oh!' he mumbled, 'I have stayed here many times in the past.' Then I invited him in and asked him if he'd like some food. His eyes lit up.

Knowing something about medicine, I warned him, 'You have to be really careful now. It's best if you eat only a little bit of food five times a day, rather than one big meal.' He looked relieved and I told him he could stay with us here. Then I gave him some food and some warm milk.

It turned out that he was an Englishman who had been in prison and had somehow escaped to the States. The prison he was sent to is famous in England. It's called Winchester gaol and is known as one of the toughest prisons in the country. I wondered what he had done to deserve this. He told me a little of his story but I did not pursue the matter. The most important thing was to get him back on his feet again.

The first day a little colour returned to his cheeks and he started to relax. He told me that he'd stayed in the Blue House on several occasions when he was a dope dealer and that our new house had been a sanctuary for him and his friends. In the trade, this is what is known as a 'safe house'.

We ended up looking after him for six months before he was really capable of doing anything. He had been very ill when he came to us and at first he was so frightened that he would scarcely go out of the house. Eventually, he told me that when he knocked on our door, he had been running from an area not far away, where there were large marijuana plantations. His work had been to guard one of these plantations, armed with a rifle. But he had got himself into big trouble there, and the people who were growing the marijuana had threatened his life. He fled in the night and thought he could come to the Blue House and hide there for a while.

Thank God nobody came looking for him. We were truly relieved because the house had become a centre for the particular work I've always been involved with: the Essence of Sufi Teachings. Our guest behaved very well and, in time, he became strong and got his health back. In return for his food and lodging, he helped us as much as he could with cleaning and garden work. He was very quiet and he never revealed any of the details of his life. We all accepted him as part of our community, and he also attended all the classes held in the house. I know he learned much about a new way of life while staying with us. He came to trust me at a level he'd never known before, and that trust was to become a turning point for him.

However, for the time being, he was in a kind of wilderness. He couldn't go back to the people he had been working with in the dope business. As he had no visa and no money, so he couldn't travel around the States, because sooner or later he would be picked up by the police. It became obvious to me that, for his own dignity and future, he had to give himself up to the authorities. After that, the past series of negative impressions could finally be redeemed, and he could start his life all over again.

One day, when he was very strong in his heart, I told him what I thought. I asked him where he had lived in England and about his family.

He replied, 'There's only my Mum. The others have all left.'

I asked him if I could telephone his mother and talk to her. He gave me a very sad look, but eventually agreed that I could call her. So, I rang his mother and explained to her what had happened.

She reacted very emotionally to my call. She argued, somewhat irrationally, that he never should have fled from prison in the first place. Then she calmed down a bit, and I suggested that I might be able to encourage him to return to England and give himself up. She was shocked, but at the same time she was very relieved.

Afterwards, I told him about the conversation with his mother and explained in great depth what I have learned about impressions, the Journey, the inner search and all the pitfalls that a seeker on the Way can encounter. And he *was* a true seeker. He was a mystic at heart and a lover of life who had just taken a step in the wrong direction.

Compassion, as far as I'm concerned means action, and it is said that the love of God is all-embracing in the Breath of His Compassion. In other words, a compassionate person does not judge, but takes action for the benefit of the people with whom he or she is working, and also for the planet as a whole.

After being together for many hours, I told him that now was the right time for him to return to England, and that I would endeavour to raise enough money for his plane fare. We shared a couple of beers, had a good meal, and then I said, 'The main problem is going to be getting you through British customs without a passport.'

'Easy,' he said, 'I will just surrender to the authorities when I arrive.'

We did manage to collect enough money for his ticket from all the friends I've worked with over the years. I watched him board the plane and that was the last I ever saw of him.

Presumably, he went back to prison. I'll never know if he ended up in another difficult situation after his prison term had been served. I only know that, through his pain and suffering, many of the younger students of our school gave up their judgmental way of seeing things, and grew into a deeper understanding of the purpose of Life.

Chapter Twenty

THE PARROT

TIME DOES NOT PASS only one way from birth to death. There are many dimensions and beautiful meanings to it, if we respect that time, like life, is given to us as a gift.

Sometimes we experience pauses in time. They are called 'intervals'. During these periods we need to have a tremendous amount of courage, perseverance and patience. I personally know of nothing more frustrating than having to sit and wait, and do nothing.

I'd been living for some years in California when it became apparent that a certain cycle had been completed. The new cycle had not yet revealed itself, and I was not sure what to do. Invitations were not piling up on my doorstep like Christmas cards in a good year. In fact, there were none. I was stuck until I finally received an invitation to go and stay on an island near Seattle. Because I had nowhere else to go, it seemed indicated that this was the correct move, and so I drove north.

When I arrived in Seattle, I ended up in a place called Port Townsend which was founded in the Victorian period by one of the Townsend family from England. He probably had been deported to America because he was a trouble-maker. Many English people were sent away to Australia or America when they became a liability to their mother country.

My wife and I first stayed in a bed and breakfast called the Victoriana Inn which had originally been a brothel when Port Townsend was a thriving fishing village. Now it had become a rather small hotel for tourists. The town had a few good restaurants and there were many artists and writers who had come to Port Townsend and made it their sanctuary. The town was very isolated. There wasn't even a regular ferry to Seattle.

I don't enjoy living as a recluse, so I rented a beautiful house with an incredible view and bought myself a small green parrot called Arthur. Arthur had been owned by a young child who fell out of love with the bird and sold him to a local store. I have noticed that all parrots are lonely, and this one was no exception, so I bought him.

I've always enjoyed walking alone, even in the rain, and in Port Townsend it rains nearly all the time. When I wanted to take a walk, there were only two ways to go: if I went one way it would lead to the yacht harbour where there was a restaurant which sold fish and chips. When I walked the other way, I would pass through Port Townsend and beyond. Every day I would walk about two miles. I was trying to write a book, hoping that my daily walks would loosen me up and create a flow. Certainly there wasn't much of a flow in Port Townsend at that time.

When I was working at my desk, the parrot would come and sit on my shoulder. Arthur was trained to be clean, so if he wanted to relieve himself and I didn't hear his inner message, he would bite my ear. All I had to do was to put Arthur in his cage, and when he had completed his task, he would come back onto my shoulder and I'd continue typing.

Communication happens on many levels. I often talk about an 'upstairs telephone number'. When you love someone very much, you will know their upstairs telephone number and they may know yours. A 'call' can come through in the form of a picture, a dream or a vision. The telephone rings and then you take action. This little parrot had very good telephone manners. I knew his number and he knew mine. I would go on a stroll, and after about two miles of meditating and walking, I would turn inside, and dial Arthur's telephone number to tell him I was coming back home.

The walk back would take me approximately twenty-five minutes. I'd tell Arthur to inform my wife that I was on my way home and so it was time to put the potatoes on for lunch. It never failed to work. The parrot, who represents the echo of thought form, would squawk loudly and my wife would hear the message. Of course Arthur didn't actually scream 'Potatoes!' But my wife, knowing that I am British and I do like potatoes, would put them on the stove and by the time I came through the door, lunch would be ready. Perhaps you've never seen a parrot smile, but when I returned from those walks, Arthur would smile and fluff up his feathers and look incredibly pleased with himself. Often I would give him a grape (he was very fond of grapes) and we would smile together and let the day unfold.

Communication is one of the most important things in life. Is there a way to communicate that isn't coloured by our preconditioned mind and our opinions? Is there a way of direct communication with one another? There is.

When the time came for us to move on, we had to give Arthur to a friend. Tony is a medical doctor and a psychologist but he didn't know much about parrots. Every morning he had to go and work at the hospital and so he had to leave Arthur alone all day long. When he came home in the evening he would greet Arthur, wash and then start reading the poetry of Mevlana Jelaluddin Rumi, the great Persian mystic. Tony said that Arthur used to coo and flutter his wings and was incredibly happy for one hour every evening while my friend read poetry to him.

Later, when I gave instructions for everyone to begin studying another thirteenth-century mystic, Tony started to read some of his work to the parrot. Arthur did not like this new sound at all and he would start screaming. Because it was necessary for Tony to go on with his studies he read out loud for one hour every evening anyway, even though Arthur continued to scream! Indeed, echoes do come back to us.

Chapter Twenty-one

TIME

Sooner or later
Time changes.
Changes from
Opinion into love.
Sooner or later
Time changes.
Can we fit into it?
Can we move with it?
Can we dance with it?
Or do we miss
The sound?
Do we miss
the moment?

THE GYPSY BASKET

WHEN I WAS a young boy I met the gypsies. My father died soon after I was born, and as I was growing up my mother was usually too busy living her own life, so most of the time she was not really there for me. However, I was never short of love because our cook loved me as her own son and cared for me.

She was a gypsy woman raised in what is called 'a family'. She left her family for some unknown reason and came to work for us as a cook. She also kept our household together in an ordered, loving and flowing way.

We had a beautiful house with acres of land in the English countryside. One year my mother allowed a family of pure Romany Gypsies to park their caravans at one end of our large estate, a place which they regarded as very special. As a young boy, I remember running to greet them. It wasn't simply a chance to escape from my own house. It was more than that. I was running towards love.

The gypsies accepted me and included me as one of the family. They had two caravans and many children with them. The children and I played together. As a young boy I shared a lot with them. They had a half-breed dog. I can see him now; we would lie down together in the grass and he'd roll around by my side. At that time, I suppose he was my best friend. The dog would sleep under one of the caravans, and they kept him on a rope so he wouldn't run off and cause trouble in the village.

One of the main things I remember about the gypsies was their extraordinary cleanliness. Their caravans were always so clean, so beautiful, so well looked after. The woman, the elder of the Family, showed me how to sit on the floor. There was a small kitchen at one end where she made us tea. I was very shy, but I trusted her completely. I shall never forget the undemanding love and total respect that she gave to me.

There came a time, though, when they had to leave. I don't know if they were asked to leave or if they wanted to leave. When gypsies start to move, there is a lot of preparation and cleaning up, so that the land is left as it was, as it should be. I still remember it so clearly. It was perhaps the loneliest time of my life. There they were packing up for the journey, while I had to stay behind. Descending the five wooden steps of the caravan and putting my feet back on the earth, I recall that if they had given me permission, I would have walked up those steps once again and gone on the road with them, forever.

I remember walking back to my house, alone, as the gypsy caravans moved on down the road, never to be seen again. It was a very sad moment, especially for an only child without many friends. I wanted so very much to go with them.

Some of my mother's friends had told me to beware of gypsies, for it is said that if you're cursed by a gypsy, you and your offspring will suffer for seven generations. But when I was with them, all that they gave to me was a lot of love. The few times I've been allowed to hold the hand of a gypsy, I felt I was holding the hand of beauty and the flow of love. I heard the wind of truth blowing through the moment.

Many, many years later, my wife and I had gone to France for a holiday. It was shortly after we had met, and she had never been to France before. I knew she had some doubts about some of the stories I had told her about my life. She listened very carefully to these stories, and because they seem to have happened almost outside of time, she was led to a state of bewilderment. Like anyone else who wants to have a true relationship with a partner, my wife needed to know whether the stories I told her were true. Were they figments of my imagination? Was I exaggerating? How can we come to know the truth about the person with whom we are sharing the journey of life? When my wife heard that I was raised by a gypsy, she was tempted to disbelieve me, so I always wanted to prove it to her somehow.

We were travelling by car through France, and I wanted to show her the Loire Valley and a famous French garden called Villandry. As we were driving to Villandry, I suddenly had a very strong intuition to go down a side road, a much narrower road than the one we were on. My wife was driving and I said, 'Slow down and turn right at the next road.'

She didn't know where we were anyway, so she didn't even question where I was leading us. Of course, I didn't know either. I was just following my intuition, without the rational mind asking why. She turned down the little road and the scenery seemed to change completely, as we found ourselves driving along a beautiful stretch of the open countryside. It was a lovely day and the grass sparkled in the sunshine.

Suddenly, as if by chance, I saw two men walking down

the road and I immediately knew they were gypsies. It was at that moment that I knew, beyond a doubt, we were driving straight into the middle of a gypsy camp. We came to three caravans parked by the side of the road. On the edge of the road a man was weaving a basket. I asked my wife to slow down, so we could have a better look. The whole scene was simply perfect: the colours, the cleanliness, the usual fire in the middle of their circle.

However, we were on our way to see the famous French garden, so we drove on. We eventually found our way to the garden. The colours were magnificent. The whole garden was an experience of order and great beauty, and we enjoyed the whole day there. The main part of Villandry is a large vegetable garden with standing rose bushes placed all around it. These rose bushes represent the monks who looked after the garden in the early part of the eighteenth century. Now they stand like sentinels watching over the vegetables growing in the sunlight. We sat in a special spot and shared a picnic in the sunshine and beauty of nature.

It was late afternoon when we eventually started back to the guest house where we were staying. I somehow managed to find that same little road where we had seen the gypsies. Down the road, sure enough, there were the gypsy caravans. We drove slowly, enchanted by the fire outside which we could see just up ahead. All of a sudden, I saw the basket which the gypsy man had been making that morning. It was sitting all alone at the edge of the road.

I said to my wife, 'Stop the car near the caravans. But you must stay in the car.'

The two dark-skinned men we had seen earlier came towards us. They looked fierce and I could see that both were carrying large knives in their belts. I looked about for the elder, the person who is really in charge of the

Family. An old woman, very short, began to walk my way. She wore the traditional Romany clothes with a long coloured skirt. I can still remember her face. Her skin was old, like parched leather. Yet inside she was shining. Then I noticed her hands. They were working hands, beautiful and strong. It's said that the hands are the extension of the heart. She walked straight to me then stopped when she was very close. She addressed me in French, with a Romany accent. The pure Romany language is close to Sanskrit, and many believe the gypsies originally came from India. Some even say that the gypsies are the Lost Tribe of Israel.

My wife remained in the car with the windows rolled up. When you deal with gypsies it is very important that everything is done in the right way, at the right time, and in the right place.

I said to the old woman, in my best French, 'There is a basket by the road. I would like to buy it. How much do you want for it?'

She then named an outrageous price, but I didn't flinch or react, as she kept her eyes locked on mine. If you ever have the opportunity to meet true gypsies, you must always look them straight in the eye. Her eyes were strong, yet gentle. I could see she would hold firm to her price. Or was she testing me? I didn't argue about the price. I just looked at her more deeply and did not waver.

Then I said, 'If you would give "the glance of the eye" to my wife who is in that car, then I will buy your basket.'

The gypsy men were hovering a short distance away, ready for anything. Here I was, challenging the old woman, the gypsy elder, and my French was very rusty so I wasn't certain if she understood 'the glance'. But my poor French didn't seem to matter, because she seemed to be able to read my thoughts.

She walked over to the car, but I did not follow. I remained motionless where I was and watched her every move. She came nearer to the car and looked in at my wife. Suddenly there was a deep silence that pervaded the whole scene and filled the atmosphere. The men were quiet. The whole family stopped what they were doing around the fire and watched. I didn't move, not one inch.

Time stood still while the old woman gave a long 'glance of the gypsies' to my wife through the closed window of the car. I could almost see the connecting space between the old gypsy woman and my wife. It seemed as though Life itself was unfolding and expanding in the inner silence. During this moment I knew that a profound change had occurred in my wife. The wise old gypsy lady walked slowly back. There were no more words between us. I gave her the money for the basket, and I still have it to this day.

If we do not understand that everything in this world has to do with relationships, then it is impossible for us to understand the purpose of life on earth. There is also a sacred relationship between the visible and invisible worlds. Without relationships there wouldn't be a world for us to experience. We can begin to understand relationships when we know that all things are interconnected and each of us is related to all of Life. In the words of Mevlana Jelaluddin Rumi,

> *I died as a mineral to become a plant,*
> *I died as a plant to become an animal,*
> *I died as an animal to become man*
> *and I will be raised still further.*

Chapter Twenty-three

A VILLAGE IN SPAIN

ONCE UPON A TIME there was a man who worked for the United Nations. This man was from an aristocratic Austrian family, stretching back generations in an unbroken line. He had many sons and before he died he appointed each one to fulfil a different function.

One of them was to go to Spain and find a village that was uninhabited which could be purchased for a reasonable amount of money. At that time there were many derelict villages which had been left empty, because the young people had all gone to the cities and the old people had moved out to live with relatives. This village would then be restored to provide a Centre where people could meet on a universal level. It was to be a place where people from all spiritual backgrounds and religions could share what they had been given and learn from one another. A village was found south of Madrid. Amphoras and ancient ruins testified that, at one time, it had been inhabited by the Romans.

I was invited there to give a seminar on geomancy and various other subjects. The community had a few horses and some cows but, unfortunately, nobody had been able to make use of them. They desperately needed to find some way of being financially self-supporting and because

I had started so many centres in my life, they asked me to give them some advice. After I had been in the village a few days, I realized there were patches of colour on the other side of the valley. I saw areas where lavender and other beautiful plants were growing and this provided the clue I needed.

At this time there was only one beehive in Torronteras. I called the community together for a meeting and said, 'Sell all the horses, sell the cows, and get more bees!'

They agreed to my plan and I suggested they design a label for the honey which would come in abundance, once sufficient bees were found. Not being a designer myself, I asked one of the brothers in the fellowship who was an artist to make a very simple design. He created a label which gave the impression of a deep sense of caring for the land. Over the next few months they worked hard, and within a year they received an award for the best honey in Spain. Over the years, orders for more and more honey have poured into the community.

There is a saying, 'Equality in Essence, but hierarchy in function'. There is a way to fulfil a useful function in life, whether as an artist, a doctor, a housewife or a husband. It doesn't really matter what we do. My teacher used to say that we have two legs – one is the leg of perseverance and the other is the leg of our predestination in eternity. We have two arms that represent wings: one is faith, and the other is belief. This means belief in a conscious awareness of our own life, and a knowledge of the function we are meant to fulfil in this life, which is lent to us for such a short period of time.

I often talk to my pupils about 'function'. I try to help them see that we must find what it is we are meant to *give back,* rather than just extracting energy from life. Life goes both ways. It is said that our Way is similar to the way of the bees, and that our house is a beehive. Bees can travel long distances in order to gather honey. They also cross-pollinate in the process. If we study the function of the bees, there is very much to be learned.

In fact, if you ever go to meet a Sufi teacher, it is appropriate to bring him or her a small pot of honey. This signifies you have been given the inner knowledge that goes with understanding our function in Life. This function is understood only by being grateful. Gratefulness is the key to Will.

Chapter Twenty-four

THREE QUESTIONS

BEING OF SERVICE in the world is often a matter of being in the right place at the right time, and doing what is needed in the moment, to the best of our ability. Over the years I have suggested to my students that they always ask three important questions before embarking on any venture or act of service.

The three questions are: May I? Should I? Can I? 'May I?' is related to Divine Will; 'Should I?' is to determine the right time; and 'Can I?' is related to one's own capability. If we ask these three questions in prayer and sincerity, and if we abide by the answer, then we will be protected from experiencing or causing unnecessary suffering.

Sometimes, however, it is difficult to know the difference between necessary and unnecessary suffering. Much of the suffering in this world is unnecessary, usually caused by one of the three walls of resentment, envy or pride. There is also necessary suffering, which brings us to the truth or which provides a needed lesson in life.

There was a time when I began to receive letters and telephone calls from a man in Germany who wanted me to give classes at a spiritual centre in Germany. He offered me a large amount of money, and although money is not of primary interest to me, I was a bit fascinated that he offered me such a large fee.

Anyway, for over a year I kept getting these letters and phone calls asking me to come to Germany. In my quiet time, I asked 'May I? Should I? Can I?' But I could not get a 'yes' to all the questions. However, he kept writing, and asking. And I kept asking, and so on. Something was not right about it all.

Then one day, after my morning prayers and meditation, when I asked the questions again, as I had just received another letter, I got three affirmatives. Therefore, I could not deny that I had to go, whatever happened. When I get a 'yes' three times I have to take action.

However I also felt that I should first meet this very persistent man. So I invited him to my home and as my guest. He agreed to come and together we shared food, wine and pleasant conversation. He seemed to be a sincere and good-hearted man, so I agreed to go to his centre in Germany and give three weeks of talks and classes. We shook hands and the agreement was sealed.

By the time I was meant to go, I was living in Seattle, and he agreed to pay the return tickets for my wife and me, as well as to pay a reasonable fee for my time and efforts. I must say, that I did not particularly want to go to Germany. Neither was I doing it for the money. I agreed only because I received a 'yes' to all the questions. When you go straight for the Truth, with both hands, you have to accept precisely what is given in the moment and then, even if the purpose of it all is inexplicable, you may later come to understand the meaning.

On the way to Germany I felt extremely nervous, but didn't know why. We arrived at the airport and looked around for someone to greet us, but nobody appeared. Surely that was a sign. We sat there at the airport and had a cup of tea, waiting to see if someone would show up. I didn't know where we were supposed to go, so we were simply stuck, waiting. Eventually, I telephoned the centre, and I asked where the driver was who was meant to meet us. Nobody seemed to have the slightest idea, and the conversation went nowhere. So there was nothing I could do but wait.

I walked around the airport, hoping someone would recognize me. Then I saw a rather strange looking man with long hair. He looked tired and not very well. I walked up to him and asked 'Have you come to meet me?' He had his head down, but then he looked up at me, rather surprised. He looked like he was in a kind of dream world, or sleep-walking. He said 'Are you Doctor Feild?'

'Yes I am!' I answered, somewhat upset after having waited in the airport for hours, not knowing what was going on. 'Do you realize,' I continued, 'that my wife and I have been waiting here for hours?'

He did not reply, but simply nodded. He didn't seem to care. Another sign! 'Please come with me,' he said, 'My car is outside.'

My wife and I gathered up our luggage and followed. The drive to the centre was over an hour, and the man offered us nothing. He hardly even spoke, and his replies to any of my questions were usually 'I don't know'. In the car there was nothing to drink, not even water. Also, the car was filthy. Another sign. If you have a guest, surely you would at least receive the guest in cleanliness and love, attention and respect.

The journey was long and I began to feel car sick, so I

asked if we could find a place to stop and have something to drink. I could sense his resentment. He did finally find a restaurant, where I ordered refreshments, which I shared with my wife, while he had an orange juice. We sat in silence.

Then we drove on, and again I got this tremendous feeling of nervousness. We drove through a forest and finally arrived at a very big house. It was one of those houses that I would imagine when watching a German opera. It was large. It was gaunt. Outside there were about thirty people sitting on the lawn. All of them seemed to be completely lost and drained of energy. The people looked at the car, and looked at us, but gave no greeting. Another sign?

We followed the driver into the house. The hallway felt empty and dark. Then someone finally did come to greet us, and she led us into a sitting room. There we sat and waited. We sat and waited for one and a half hours. We were offered some stale cheese, which was sweating badly, and a jug of water. We waited and waited, expecting our host to appear any minute.

Finally I got up from the sofa, leaving my wife alone with the cheese, and almost ran into the main area of the house, shouting 'What the hell is going on? Where is the man who invited me?'

A woman appeared and said, 'He is praying.'

I said, 'Then stop him praying and get him down here, right now!' I then stormed out of the room and returned to my wife. There we waited for another twenty minutes. Then finally the man who had invited me, walked into the room. He was wearing an off-white silk robe, lined with gold. This took me by surprise, because when he had visited me he was always dressed immaculately in a suit and tie. With him was a huge man, a bodyguard, who could have swept me under his feet with one kick.

I stood up from the couch and took a deep breath, 'I am very upset,' I said, 'You have been very rude. Why did you invite me here and then not even greet me when I arrive? You made us wait at the airport. You made us wait here. Don't you think that we might be tired after such a long journey? You're involved with a spiritual centre, but you can't even consider your guest.'

The man in the robes made a small apology, but I didn't feel he was sincere. He took us upstairs to the room where my wife and I were to stay. The room seemed to have a strange odour which I couldn't recognize. My wife then went in to see the bathroom that was next to the bedroom. She came back so fast, it was like a rocket bouncing off the planet Mars.

'I will NOT go in there!' she said, looking at me to show that her word was final.

When a woman is adamant about something, you need to pay heed. My wife is very intuitive and can sense things that most people cannot. I was curious as to what she meant, so I had a look. It had a marble floor and was actually quite an extraordinary bathroom, but there was something subtle and foreboding about it. It was impossible to explain why. The atmosphere completely overwhelmed both of us, and there was an air of cruelty and violence which pervaded every single stone and even the marble floor. More than that I did not know at the time.

I told the host that this room was not appropriate for us, and of course, I felt his resentment. We did stay there that night after all. It was the only spare bedroom in the large house; however, we heard of an old inn within walking distance, to which we moved the next day.

That night I had promised to give a lecture in the main house. Again, I felt an odd energy in the house. It lacked anything to do with love or the work of transformation. Something was definitely wrong, and I began to feel that we should leave this place, as soon as possible.

On that very night, at around eleven-thirty when I was already in bed, there was a knock on the door. My wife and I were summoned to some important meeting. I thought it was quite ridiculous to have a meeting so late in the night, but I was told that I must go – for the meeting was about me!

There were about thirty people in the dimly lit room, in two half-moon circles, and I was placed in front of them. Soon I realized that this was an Inquisition! They accused me of being an impostor. It turned out that all the people there were Muslim converts. I can respect that, but I do not believe that one must convert to anything, in order to follow the Way of Love and Truth. I'd rather become a true human being, than follow any set dogma. But they accused me of breaking their spiritual rules, of drinking alcohol and not praying at the right time, etc, etc. It was not surprising that they had certain bad opinions about me. Over the years I have become used to people judging me for one thing or another. It is the price any teacher has to pay.

What I found surprising, though, was that my host already knew all this about me when he first invited me to this place! He had even come to stay in my house, where we had wine and had talked about such matters. He never said he was an Orthodox Muslim. So there was something quite dishonest in all these accusations. Had they invited me here, only to punish me in some way? I thought back to all the many signs on this peculiar journey. From the very beginning, something seemed to be wrong. So, did I make some mistake in asking the three questions, or in receiving the answers? If not, then why was I made to suffer in this way? Maybe for my own learning? Maybe for theirs? Or maybe there was some action that needed to take place here, in order to transform or redeem certain patterns of the past? So, what now? I listened, but said nothing. I did not react. I just breathed and waited until it was over.

The next day I told the people at the centre that I could not stay any longer. I said that I did not want any of the money promised to me, and that all I really wanted was to get out of there and go home. I asked them to provide a car and driver, to take me to the train station. But they refused. They argued that I had made an agreement to stay there, and that I should honour the agreement. It was true I had made an agreement, but I felt danger and a sense of darkness in the place. I had to get out of there. But how could I without their help? We were stuck in the middle of this forest with no bus, taxis, or anything.

I walked from the inn to the main house to have some breakfast, which consisted of a cup of coffee and a piece of bread. The inn provided no food. From the window I saw an old man working in the garden. He must have been about seventy years old. I thought that he might know some of the history behind this place. So I went out and tried to talk to him, but he didn't speak English.

Nonetheless, I tried to communicate, gesturing here and there, but it was no use. So I returned to sit with my coffee and watched the old gardener at work.

I knew, intuitively, that this very place had a history that still lingered on within its walls. Something strange must have happened, and something strange was still going on. What was it? Surely, the gardener would know, I thought, for he must have been around during the last war.

Just then, a man in a business suit arrived and sat down at my table. He introduced himself as the attorney for the man who had invited me. He told me that I owed the centre a lot of money for causing so much distress, and that if I left before the three weeks were up, I would owe them even more money.

It was incredible! I had already told these people that I did not want any of their money, and now they were trying to get every bit of savings I had! I told the man in the suit that *they* were the ones causing the distress. All I wanted was to get out of here and go back home. I told him to take me to court if he wanted, but I would leave, one way or another.

He finally left, and I never saw him again. I finished my coffee and resumed watching the old gardener. Then, in one of those sudden flashes, when time zones collide, I saw soldiers of the German Nazi army coming towards me, with their high boots, walking like robots with great precision. At the same time I saw a column of tired English soldiers, who had obviously suffered for a long time, walking the other way. I was seeing two time zones at once, one during the war and the other just after! I also knew that the Nazi soldiers had been involved with something very inhumane in this very place. I could see terrible experiments going on and heard screams and pleas for mercy. It was all in a flash, a flash of seeing through time.

When I returned to the present, my body was shaking from this nightmare and I felt sick in my stomach. What I had seen was not a fantasy. It was as real as the gardener working in front of me. I felt agitated. Had this house been involved with something that was not a part of real living? What went on here, years ago? And what is going on here now? These were my thoughts, my questions. Had I seen into the past, or seen into what was repeating itself in the present? How is the past related to the present? Does time repeat itself, unless the past is redeemed? And, what can I possibly do now, to help the future? There were so many questions to consider.

I went to the office of this centre and again asked if they could possibly get a car and a driver to take us to the railway station. Again, they absolutely refused to do anything. So I went back to the inn and told my wife to pack our suitcases. We would find some way out of here. I remembered the name of a certain German couple who had once written me a lovely letter of thanks, after reading my first two books, and I thought that possibly they could help us. I asked the manager of the inn to call information and track down their telephone number. Success! The husband happened to be home, and he was very warm and friendly. I felt relieved already.

He couldn't come himself, but he did know of someone close by who, as it turned out, was an old friend of mine giving a seminar not far away from where we were. Now things were moving!

I called this nearby friend and asked, even begged him to come and collect us. He did, that day, and drove us to the station, where my wife and I took a train to Holland to recover from our ordeal.

Yet I still wanted to find out what the gardener knew. The couple in southern Germany, whom I had called to rescue us, invited us to stay with them for a while at their home. She worked as a homeopath, and he managed finances in a large company. He was a mystic, in essence, but in the outer form he was just a normal businessman. When we were having supper together, I asked him 'Do you know anybody in German Intelligence?'

This is not a question to usually ask anyone, and you cannot really expect an answer. He looked intently at me, but said nothing. There was quite a long pause. I had an intuition that he *did* know someone.

Breaking the silence, I said 'I don't expect you to answer that, but . . . if you know any young person who could go to that centre disguised, as it were, as some sort of spiritual hippie, then perhaps some good could come out of that visit.'

We had no further conversation on this matter, but I felt that something might be done. My wife and I went back to the States, and a few months later I received a letter in the post and a copy of a leading magazine in Germany. In this magazine there was a major article on this so-called spiritual centre. Many things had been found out and exposed. It confirmed what I'd seen and what I'd felt. And I was right, the gardener knew everything.

The house had indeed been used in the last war for genetic experiments, which included working on gypsies,

Jews and animals, and the nearby inn had been a centre for the Nazi secret police, the SS. The really interesting point was not the fact that it had been used for such activities; after all, many such things have taken place in war time that no one would be particularly proud of. What was important to me was that the vibration and memory remained within the house itself, and because of my own state of sensitivity I was able to tune into a whole series of events that had happened sometime in the past.

The article also exposed some of the fanaticism and psychological manipulation going on at the present time. Sometime later, after receiving this article, I heard that the centre had been closed down.

Reading the article, and learning about the history of the place, I wondered again why I had ever become involved with it all. If I hadn't received a 'yes' to all three questions, I would never have gone. So why did I get a 'yes' three times? Maybe I needed to learn something. Maybe they needed to learn something. Maybe I was necessarily involved with a transformation and redemption of the past. Maybe there were many reasons.

Chapter Twenty-five

ROBES

A LONG TIME AGO I wore robes for about two years. Everybody thought I was completely crazy, because I was walking around in robes made by Pierre Cardin! My under-robe had eighteen blue buttons representing the eighteen tests in the Sufi tradition and I went around in bare feet and sandals.

During this time I flew to New York. I arrived at Kennedy airport and went through customs. In those days you could see through the glass windows, looking down on every single person, and there I was, looking like a Franciscan monk. And I had been met by a young friend who had long red hair down to his waist, wearing purple velvet. The customs official had a big cigar in his mouth and he was huge. He made me open all the suitcases and all the people were watching. I had every one of the Bach Flower Remedies with me, which I have always used for healing purposes. They all look identical, and I had a large quantity of homeopathic remedies with me also. The huge customs official picked up one of the homeopathic remedies and asked,

'What's that?'
I said, 'Well it's a sort of *"like treats like"*.'

That was a stupid way to answer.

Then he picked up a bottle of Bach Remedies, all looking identical – there were thirty-eight of them in all – and he said he had to analyze it and the homeopathic remedies also. I waited about ten or fifteen minutes. He came back, handed me a homeopathic remedy and said,

'This responds to cocaine.'

I said, 'It can't respond to cocaine, it's homeopathy.'

Then he asked, 'What's this?' pointing at the Bach Flower bottle he had previously picked up.

I answered, 'Mimulus.'

'What's that for?' he asked.

'Fear,' I replied.

'Are you frightened?' he asked.

At this point my whole body was sweating – the robes from Pierre Cardin were rather heavy. It turned out he was bluffing, so he did eventually let me go. As I started to walk out of the glass doors I got stopped by a man flashing a CIA badge at me. He asked me to follow him. The only thing I had in my pocket, apart from a little bit of money, was my prayer beads. They were taken away for testing in an X-ray machine. I said, 'Those are my prayer beads.'

There was a big man with a huge cigar and a smaller man in the room. They asked me to take my clothes off and I was body-searched. They never apologized, ever. They went through all the suitcases and then through me and never apologized. I walked out and met my friend who had also been searched.

The man in purple velvet had presumed that we would be staying at the house of a famous French-American actress. That didn't work out so my friend said, 'I know some people who have a barge.' It was on Staten Island. We drove there, and at the edge there was a bar on one side and a parking lot on the other. Then there was a gang-plank leading to the barge. I was exhausted – I'd just arrived from England in full robes.

We walked onto the gang-plank, and when we arrived inside there were about seventy-five people sitting on the floor and in the middle there was a man with a vast Chinese gong, sitting on a Chinese sort of chair. As I came in, on the left-hand side there were about five bowls, all full of pills. They were vitamins B and C and they were all eating handfuls of them. I stood at the threshold and looked at all these people. Suddenly a woman screamed, 'Aaaaah', a bit like the primal scream. She screamed and the man hit the gong and said, 'Elizabeth is enlightened!' At this point everybody got up, surrounded her and hugged her.

I just couldn't take it. I suggested to Leonard, my friend, that we go and have a drink. So we went to the bar by the parking lot. He was dressed in purple velvet with red hair down to his waist, and I was in Franciscan robes, and we walked into the bar. Of course, everybody stared at us. About twenty minutes later I could see fire coming through the window. I thought, 'Oh dear, my robes will catch fire!' A man came in with wide eyes, looking completely crazy, – he had just set the parking lot on fire by lighting up a few cars! Then the police came and I said, 'We'd better go back to the barge.'

Someone showed me to my cubicle. I remember going in – it was quite small – taking off the robes, keeping just my underpants on and getting into bed. I thought, 'There's something strange going on here, I'm not alone.'

I felt sure there was someone in my bed. First of all I wanted to know if the presence was male or female. It was pitch-black and I felt it was a female presence. She was awake. I asked, 'What the hell are you doing in my bed?'

There was no answer. Nothing happened because I refused, and I did manage to sleep a bit. When the dawn came, I saw the lady was incredibly beautiful and it turned out she was a well-known New York yoga teacher.

Certainly this was a time of my life which many people who knew me found extremely difficult to understand. But it contained so much humour and pathos that I was eventually helped to see the need to move on. It was around this time I decided to take off my robes forever.

Chapter Twenty-six

FAITHFUL IN LIFE

What does it mean to be faithful in life?
To be faithful is not what it appears to be.
As Jesus said, faithfulness starts with thought.
When we are faithful to the moment,
then we will not be faithful
to anything outside of that moment.
If we can see the stars, the moon,
and the wind moving through the trees,
it is impossible to be unfaithful to life.
Can we see each moment,
can we hear each moment,
can we receive the meaning of each moment?
Can we be faithful, in life, and to life, each moment?

Chapter Twenty-seven

THE BLACK CHRIST

IT'S TRULY AMAZING how the universe provides all the teaching we need, as long as we can look to the signs. Looking to the signs does not mean projecting onto life what we want of it, but rather reversing space, and coming to realize that what we see in the outer world is a reflection of what is within ourselves, or what we need to know at any one moment.

I was invited to come to New York to bring together many different spiritual groups who were in fierce competition with one another. At that time, there was a lot of spiritual ambition in the air. People thought that, instead of bringing their inner work to daily life, there was actually some 'alternative' to normal living.

I accepted the invitation on certain conditions. One of them was that no group could advertise what they were doing. It was my intention that we would all come together and spend a day of sharing without comparison. It turned out to be a tremendous day for everybody and we finished up by chanting and praying together in the Oneness of Being.

That evening, I was packing up my things to return home when a friend called, saying 'Reshad, would you like to meet the Black Christ?'

'Pardon me?' I replied, 'What on earth do you mean?'

I was rather bewildered, so he went on to explain that a very famous teacher, now deceased, had met this Black American and decided that he was the reappearance of Christ. Before he died, he told all his followers to go and see him.

This was too tempting, so I made the decision to cancel my plane ticket and told my friend that I would like to visit this Black Christ as soon as possible.

'Meet me in one hour,' he said.

Then I hurried off to the local store where I bought some fruit and had it nicely wrapped, hoping that this would be a suitable gift for a Black Christ. My friend picked me up in his car and we went off into the night.

Soon, I noticed that something was very peculiar. I'd imagined that a 'Christ', black or white, would be living in a decent area, but we were driving straight into the slums. I had never seen such poverty and destitution. It was really appalling. Eventually, we turned into a back street littered with broken-down cars and I was informed that we had reached our destination. My English sense of humour took over and I wondered if we were going to find the Black Christ holding court in the back seat of one of these abandoned cars!

Instead, we entered a small house just off the alley and went up some rickety stairs straight into a kitchen jammed with people. It was so crowded we couldn't move. Off to one side, there was a large stove with three enormous cooking pots, which were steaming away and giving off a dreadful smell. There was no sign of any Christ whatsoever, but when I looked into the people's eyes, I noticed they were filled with light.

Finally, somebody asked, 'Would you like to see him now?'

'Yes, please,' I replied, eyeing the cooking pots suspiciously.

They led us out of the kitchen and down a passageway to a tiny bedroom. A black gentleman was sitting on the bed, munching on a sandwich and watching the football game on television. He did not look very special to me. But then, who really knows who is who, anyway? Sitting on the bed next to him was a rather beautiful woman who, I found out later, was a prostitute. She had come to him for healing. At first, he didn't seem to take any notice of her. I didn't know what to do, so I sat on the floor and tried to look humble. My friend also sat on the floor and tried to look humble.

I could see that the bedsheets hadn't been changed for a long time, and I had to keep myself from judging him. After all, who are we to judge? The game on TV came to an end and he finished his sandwich. He turned to the woman sitting on the edge of the bed.

He looked carefully into her eyes and with a loud voice he shouted out, 'Red medicine'. Then he grabbed her by the shoulders and shook her like jelly. He moved his hands a little lower and shook her even more. 'Now, go and get your medicine,' he said. I must say that when she got off the bed, she looked amazingly different.

Suddenly, he looked at me and said, 'You!'

'Yes?' I answered meekly. I hadn't come to see the Black Christ for healing, I felt perfectly well, actually.

He looked at me briefly and ordered, 'White medicine only.' He turned back to the TV and that signalled the end of our meeting.

My friend and I returned to the kitchen. A huge man was attending the bubbling pots. He smiled broadly. 'The Black Christ told me to have the white medicine,' I offered humbly.

'Ahhh,' he replied with a comforting tone, 'With the white medicine, you'll only be on the toilet for twenty-four hours; with the red, it's three days and the black is one week!'

He explained they were herbs from Africa and that I should have a look inside the pots. Holding my nose, I peeked inside them, and saw that one contained white medicine, one red and one black. Before he gave me the medicine, he added a few other ingredients. I watched him carefully. First, he added a bottle of American white port wine and then a bit of rosé. The concoction bubbled away and the smell in the room became even worse. Eventually, he completed the mix and handed me my bottle of white medicine.

When I arrived back at the house where I was staying, I asked myself, 'What is this really all about? Is he really a healer? Is he a fraud? Is he actually doing good for people? Or is it simply through *agreement* that his healings seem to work?' Later I discovered that, indeed, they did work and many people were helped. I also found out that he was a car mechanic by trade and that's why his sheets were so dirty! His hands were covered in car oil!

One of the lessons I learned from this story is that the word *agreement* is a stronger word than God – in a relative sense. It is truly amazing what we can accomplish, simply by agreeing that all things are possible. Because this man was given such a tremendous amount of agreement through the introduction by a very famous spiritual leader, it helped people to believe in the healing process. On the other hand, I believe that this man *did* have an extraordinary healing ability and thus benefited many people on the road.

Chapter Twenty-eight

THE SHEIKH

WHEN I RETURNED HOME, I received a phone call from a man who told me he was a Sufi Sheikh of a particular Order. He spoke impeccable English but I did notice a trace of an accent. He informed me that he had read my first book and wanted to meet me.

He invited me to his home but would not say exactly where it was. I was told to drive to a certain town, about two hours from where I lived, then follow a specific road for a certain distance where there would be a lay-by along the road to park the car. Here we were supposed to wait for a dark blue Mercedes to arrive and lead us to the house. The invitation was quite bizarre, I thought, with all these complicated directions. I was thinking that maybe he didn't ever give his address to strangers, and of course, he didn't actually know me yet.

On the appointed day, I began this journey with my wife and a young American student who was visiting me at the time. We arrived at the agreed spot a few minutes early and waited. Then, exactly at the agreed time, a large blue Mercedes arrived. It was spotlessly polished and appeared to be brand new. The driver was alone. He looked East Indian and wore a black cap, so I assumed he was a professional chauffeur. He didn't get out of the Mercedes but merely motioned with his hand for us to follow him in our car. We followed the large Mercedes for about twenty minutes. Soon we didn't have a clue where we were. I did notice that we were driving through a very wealthy area, with huge houses and large estates. Finally we went down a private driveway and came to a stop. There was a huge iron gate, which suddenly opened to let us through. We followed and soon we arrived at a very beautiful and large house.

A man was waiting outside to greet us, but I knew he wasn't the Sheikh. He politely reached out his hand and said, 'Welcome Doctor Feild, I hope the drive was pleasant. Our Sheikh is preparing himself to meet you and of course we have prepared some food for lunch.'

He greeted my wife and then said, 'The women enter the house from the other side.' A woman in traditional Islamic clothes appeared as if from nowhere. She greeted my wife, then asked her to follow, as my friend and I were led into the house through the front door.

It all happened so quickly that I barely had time to say anything to my wife, as she was whisked away. My wife is usually right beside me when we make social visits, so it seemed rather odd that she went one way and I the other, but in respect to my host I did not argue. Anyway, I knew she would be fine and I expected to see her soon enough.

Inside the house was a lovely atmosphere, with Middle Eastern art pieces complementing a more Western style of furnishing. We were shown into a sitting room where we very politely sat and waited for the Sheikh to arrive. I hadn't the slightest idea what to expect or what would happen. And I didn't have any idea who this man was, how he might look, or what on earth we would talk about. I didn't even know why he'd invited me. And I still had no idea where my wife was. On the table was a plate of dates and Turkish apricots. My American friend looked longingly at these dishes, but just as he reached out, I grabbed his arm and insisted that he did not eat a thing until he was invited to do so. In fact, I told him to sit quietly and not even open his mouth unless he was asked to speak. I explained to him that we should behave properly as good guests.

Very soon our host appeared, and we immediately rose from our couch to greet him. He was about my height and looked around my age. His eyes were clear and radiant, and he wore a simple Islamic robe. By now I knew he must be a Muslim who followed the laws of the Koran. There was an immediate closeness between us. All I can say is that it felt very extraordinary. I had brought him a small gift, for it is always good manners to bring your host a special gift. He accepted it graciously.

The Sheikh was a man of incredible dignity, yet carried an air of humbleness. We met in our eyes and in our hearts. There was a kind of instant recognition. My heart sang in his presence. The respect between us was absolutely and completely sincere. I was saying thank you for inviting us, and he kept saying thank you for coming.

I don't remember all that we talked about, though I do remember how grateful I felt to be conversing and sharing with a human being of such dignity and presence. He was born in Iraq and had studied there with a certain Sufi Sheikh, who was the Head of a particular Order. Before this teacher died, he designated my host to be the new leader of the Order. As my host shared some things about himself, I knew that he was not an idle man. He had started a few centres in Pakistan, a centre in England, and one in America. He was also very busy with many projects and he had even built some hospitals in Pakistan for the poor. He also owned many businesses in trade and commerce. He didn't mention how he had acquired his wealth, yet I knew he must have been a multi-millionaire.

At one point he looked at my American friend and picked up the plate of dried fruit and offered them. The American gratefully chose a date. Later on, a man came in bringing many plates of different foods. The Sheikh asked us to sit down with him for a meal in the next room. Suddenly I remembered my wife. Where was she, and why was she not invited to this special meal? Just as I was thinking this, the Sheikh said,

'Oh, your wife. You must be wondering where she is. She is with the women. She is with my wives. I know this must seem strange to you, and I am not being rude, but it is part of our Islamic custom that the men meet with men and the women meet with women. But don't worry, she is just fine, and the two of you will be reunited soon after our meal.'

I felt sorry that she could not share this experience with me. But of course, I was the guest and it is right that the guest should accept the particular customs of his host. During our meal it suddenly dawned on me that this was a week of Ramadan, which in the Islamic tradition is a time of fasting. Now I was really puzzled. Everything I'd seen and everything he'd said, pointed to the conclusion that he was a devout Muslim and followed the Koran to the very letter. Yet why was he eating food with us? I asked him,

'My dear friend, I do not wish to be impolite, but I was assuming you were a devout Muslim.'

He replied, 'Yes, I am.'

'But,' I said, 'Isn't this the time of Ramadan, the time of fasting?'

'Of course it is,' he replied, 'I was wondering if you knew this. You must be wondering why I am eating with you. I'm sharing food with you because you are my guest. It would be rude to invite you here without offering you food, and it would be rude for you to eat this food when your host cannot. I cannot, by the Law, eat food on the days of fasting, but this is not the Law you have chosen to follow. We believe that man must make his own choice, to submit to the Law set by God, or not. I do not wish to break a law of the Holy Koran, but at the same time I must not break the laws of manners in friendship. If you had refused to eat the food, because of Ramadan, then we would fast together, but you are eating and so I eat with you.'

I was still confused. 'Yet what about breaking the law?' I asked. 'Are you not still breaking the law?'—

'No, actually I am not,' he smiled and took a bite of food. 'For it says in the Holy Koran that if a man has travelled for "more than fifty miles" in one day, he can then have something to eat and drink, even in the days of fasting. I suppose that after travelling such a distance, he would need a bit of food and drink. So, since I knew you were coming, and I thought you might not be an orthodox

Muslim, I had my chauffeur drive me for over fifty miles before you arrived.'

He smiled. And so did I.

During this special time together we talked about our experiences along the path. It was somewhat like a game of cat and mouse, as we each wanted to learn more about each other, but our questions, as well as our answers, were usually indirect and never quite to the point. There was a kind of playfulness in our discovery of each other. Yet at the same time, the meeting felt deeply profound.

At one point, I couldn't help but ask him about his wives, for he had mentioned wives and not wife. He had three. This was accepted in his tradition and by the Law of the Koran. He told how he met each of his wives and admitted that each of them was very different. It turned out I had met one of his wives when I was writing my second book in Hawaii. She used to attend the story sessions. She was English and a company manager. The Sheikh had seen her and immediately fallen in love, so he purchased the company in which she worked and proposed to her after a business dinner!

Eventually it was time to leave. About three hours had passed, and finally my wife reappeared. Naturally, I wondered what she had been doing all this time. The Sheikh handed her a gift and apologized for not being able to invite her in with the men. He explained that such separation of the sexes was the custom of his tradition. I could see that my wife respected this. I realized that my wife's experience, in the last hours, must have been quite special and unique in its own right.

We all parted company in a sound of gratefulness. The

chauffeur drove in front of us to lead us out of the estate and onto the right road home. There would be other times, over the years, when the Sheikh and I would meet. Every time was a blessing. He was important to me in a way I cannot describe. It has something to do with a man's loneliness along the road and the rarity of meeting someone who feels like a close brother. Maybe because he was also a teacher and healer and had understood within himself the essence of Divine Truth.

Yet one day we had to part company. On the outer level our friendship divided, though on the inner level our love together will always be, just as it was in the very beginning. The division was about what appeared to be an irresolvable difference between us. He followed a certain way and certain fixed rules. I respected his beliefs, but his way was not necessarily *my* way. In essence there is only one true Way, but in form there are many.

I believe the dignity of Man lies in his true freedom, the freedom to be true to himself, but not necessarily within a given form. To me, the perfect and right form is whatever is needed in the moment, whatever is needed in love, and whatever can help fufil the destiny of man. This can only be known in one moment of time, which is this very moment, right now, which is the only moment there is.

So I know, in essence, there never will be any separation between the Sheikh and myself. I'll always love this man as I love the ground upon which I stand.

Chapter Twenty-nine

PARACHUTE PAM

NOTHING IN LIFE is really logical, or totally sequential as we might wish it to be. Surprises live in pain or joy. Personally I have always felt that without humour, life would be almost impossible. And do not humour and timing go together?

Laughter is a great healer. There is little or no laughter on the in-breath! We take our impressions on the in-breath and then laugh on the out-breath. We can laugh until the tears pour down our cheeks, and our jaws ache. And why should humour be anything separate from our spiritual journey?

Every year, on my birthday, I used to invent a new play in my own theatre of life. I would invite many friends, and even total strangers. It could be said that we were playing out what was pouring forth from the present moment of time. I merely set some sort of stage. The ambiance was always good, surprises were always hovering in the air, and there was the feeling that it was everyone's birthday. Wherever I was I tried to make that day, the day of my birth, a celebration. After all, we only have one real birthday, the day we come into this world.

Many years ago, when I was living in England, I was

living in a converted mill house in the south-western part of England. I had decided to give the usual crazy, and I hoped funny, birthday party. I devised a 'spiritual treasure hunt' and put up clues as to the direction people were meant to take when they were driving their cars along the narrow English country lanes. Many of the guests had been working with me in what we sometimes call The Path of Transformation, and so surprises, as such, were nothing new to them.

There were eighteen clues written on pieces of paper and hidden in unlikely places for the guests to find. Each one did provide some sort of a sign concerning the journey of life, but all with a great sense of humour. There was even a local village called *Turkdean* which naturally gave me a wonderful opening to the next place they should stop. No, it wasn't that they should actually go to Turkey, but the next clue was written on small pieces of paper in a telephone box in the middle of the heart of the English countryside.

The words were, 'The Shaykh likes trout', and then, since everyone had been given a very detailed map of the area, those who were in tune to the moment were able to find a trout farm some miles away, and when they eventually returned, they had all brought fresh trout with them. I was already there wearing a white apron and a chef's hat, ready to cook what they had brought from their journey.

The spring weather was exceptionally good. The garden was full of singing birds, the river was flowing, and the party went on for a long time. Many musicians came and they played their hearts out. Then the time approached when the gathering simply had to end, and little by little the people began to drift away and return home.

The sun was going down and the shadows moved across the lawn and the gardens. All of the party crowd had gone but there was one car still parked by the river. Whose car was it? Where could they have gone?

Directly in front of me was a river with a dirt track leading up into the hills. I was concerned about whose car it was, so I made some enquiries. I found out later that the car belonged to a woman called Pam, whom I had re- named Parachute Pam. Before I met her, Parachute Pam was jumping out of aeroplanes to raise money for the poor people of the world. (I don't jump out of aeroplanes, but I do the same thing in another way.) One time, she jumped out of a plane and her parachute didn't open. She broke both her legs horribly. It was a miracle that she had sur- vived at all and was still alive to come to my party.

When I looked in the car I noticed it was rigged for a disabled person. 'Oh, dear,' I said to myself, remembering that I had met Parachute Pam earlier in the day. I was a bit worried because on the other side of the river there was a small lake which had become a quagmire. It was so dan- gerous that it was completely enclosed in barbed wire and none of the locals would go near it. There were many sto- ries about people who had mysteriously disappeared. Had she fallen into the swamp?

It was starting to get dark. What would you do? Well, in England the answer is: Call the police! I waited for an- other hour and then I called them. I told him, 'I just had a big party and one of my guests is missing. The lady has left her car behind and she's disabled.'

Shortly thereafter three policemen arrived and I explained the situation to them. One of the policemen was very upset because he wanted to be at home with his wife. They searched for Parachute Pam until two in the morning. Finally they said, 'We give up. We will return at dawn.'

By this time, my wife was furious with me. It was two-thirty in the morning and we still hadn't been to bed. Even though I didn't really know this particular guest, I was doing all that I could to make sure that she was safe and sound. Is this not compassion? Should we not always try to remember this?

Suddenly, I heard a tremendous uproar moving down the road. It was a fleet of armoured cars. It seemed a whole army was arriving. I swallowed hard as I watched about twenty or thirty highly armed men come out of each truck. To my surprise, they were camouflaged with branches and leaves so they looked like walking trees. I was told they were going off to search the banks of the river and the surrounding area.

They continued to rummage around for about three hours. Then the police came, dressed in blue and wearing all sorts of medals. I didn't know what to do with all these people marching about. So, being practical, I made sandwiches and gave them all a cup of tea. Always offer the English a cup of tea in emergencies! The soldiers walked three miles down the river, they walked three miles up the river, and they walked in the middle of the river, too! The soldiers returned from scouring the countryside, got back into their trucks, and left.

I had a neighbour called John. He was a highly sensitive man who had the ability to tune into the moment and he was able to find anything at all through his highly attuned inner senses. In England such people are called 'Dowsers'. He had come up to the house to see what all the commotion was about. Naturally in the wilds of the countryside, the sight of men, all dressed up in camouflage walking up and down the river at first light, closely followed by a small army of police, was irresistible. I imagine that people from miles around were already up and about, trying to find out what was going on. After all, not too much happens in a small village like this.

'What on earth is going on?' John asked.

I did my best to explain. I told him that the police came first of all, stayed until early in the morning, then gave up and said that they would have to call in the special branch of the army. Thus these men, all dressed like trees, were searching for someone who had disappeared.

'John', I said, 'Please, with your psychic abilities, can you find this woman, dead or alive?' I was truly worried now.

The special brigade of the army had, by this time, walked the three and a half miles down the river to the nearest village. Perhaps Pam had drowned and been swept away. The pub opened early so everyone could come and witness. The bus drivers, who only came about twice a day, stopped everything. Everyone stared in total amazement.

Back at the big house I waited, and waited. The head of police was furious. I offered him and his team still more tea. He was not amused, and at that precise moment John came back in his little French car which was coughing and spluttering!

'I've found them,' he said, triumphantly.

'*Them*?' I replied, 'Who are *they*?'

John told me the story. He had sat quietly by himself– and in all the commotion this could not have been easy – but he asked to be guided to where this woman might be if, indeed, she was still alive. He drove his car about four miles in the direction he had intuitively felt.

He found her! Apparently Parachute Pam had met up with a wild Irishman who was cycling around the world. He had just read one of my books and had found his way to my door almost as if by accident. The two of them had been attracted to one another, and had slipped off together unnoticed. When John found them, they were curled up under the walls of a fourteenth-century castle, in a sleeping bag, with a thermos flask of tea beside them. So, while a full brigade of police and half an army were out looking for them, they were blissfully unaware of everything that had been going on!

When John returned I asked him to go back, once again, to Parachute Pam and the Irish round-the-world cyclist, and tell them to come back – 'Right now,' I said vehemently. Some time later a rather odd-looking group of three returned to the house. The army had gone, but the police were still there, shuffling their hands, and the head of police was most definitely cross. His hair was all electric and standing up under his hat which, almost perceptibly, moved.

'Enough is enough,' he said. I remember his voice was rather quiet. The Colonel was breathing hard, I was trying not to laugh at the whole situation, and the rest of the police were wanting to go back for a late breakfast.

'Now you two,' he said, addressing the couple, 'Please sign this report. And remember,' he raised himself to his full height, 'You are not the only people in the world.'

No further words were spoken. Parachute Pam and the Irish bicyclist signed the paper, and, very quietly, we all went on our way.

Chapter Thirty

THE LABRADOR

ONCE UPON A TIME, in my younger days, I was invited to a large party in England. The house was so big that the ballroom could hold four hundred people, and the lady who owned it was very wealthy. The champagne was flowing in every direction, the butlers were running around in circles, and the guests danced late into the night. Personally, I was rather bored.

At some point I left behind all the noise and went upstairs to find a room, with the hope of getting a night's sleep. I laid down on the bed and went fast to sleep. Suddenly I was awakened by a loud knocking on the door. The door wasn't locked, so I called out for whoever it was to just come in. It was the owner of the house. She was very upset. Her dog had just been run over on the private driveway. His back was broken, and he was bleeding from both ends. She had heard that I was known to have some healing ability and asked me to help. So I very quickly got dressed and ran downstairs.

A car and chauffeur were waiting outside, and I was rushed off to where the dog lay. It was a Black Labrador. The poor dog lay there on the side of the long driveway, badly bleeding and in great pain. I was extremely tired, but I wanted to help in whatever way I could. The owner was in tears. The dog was very precious to its owners, and they loved him like a child. It was a beautiful dog.

Many people were watching but not knowing what to do. Someone said there might be an ambulance on the way. Others spoke of rushing him to the hospital. But nobody really took any action. They just watched. To me, the answer seemed obvious at the time. Put one hand at one end of the dog and put the other hand at the other end and pray! And that's what I did! I breathed in love and I breathed out love. This absolute flow of love poured through the dog. Then a very amazing thing happened. I felt the dog's back turn straight. In those moments of love, I watched as the dog's broken back began shifting and fitting back into place. I'd never seen anything like this in my life. The back literally came back to itself. I also noticed that the bleeding had stopped. All this happened within minutes.

I then encouraged the dog to move. I was on my knees saying, 'Come on boy. You can do it. You can get up. You can move.'

Little by little the Black Labrador started to move. He moved a little, then a little more, then some more, until finally he got up on his legs. The people started cheering him on, clapping and yelling, 'You can do it boy. You can do it.' He looked around. He knew he was loved. I had moved away by now, giving him some room to walk. He looked at me and walked over to me. I gave him a big hug, not worrying about getting blood on my clothes. Then the owners rushed over to hug and kiss their precious Black Labrador.

I'm sure that many of the guests stayed up even later

that night, but I went back to my room to get some sleep. I got out of my clothes and washed the blood off my hands. Then I fell fast asleep, feeling ever so grateful, in absolute humility, that I was allowed to help on the Road of Truth. His back never did grow completely straight again, so his walk was always crooked but he lived until he was thirteen years old.

Healing can occur on many levels. The physical body, the energy body, the emotional body. There is mental healing. And there is healing our connection with the Source. There are also different techniques of healing. . . .

Some time later, I met a man called Max Busby who lived in England. When we met I felt an intense presence of honesty within him. He was a natural healer and once a year he would go to the ocean to collect some pebbles. They later came to be known as 'Busby pebbles'. People from all walks of life came to see him, and they usually arrived with some ailment or another. He would give the person a pebble which, in some unknown way, had absorbed the healing force that had passed through his hands. He told the person to keep the pebble in his or her pocket. Just one pebble was enough. . . .

I'M A LOVER

I am a very dangerous man.
I am a lover.
A lover is someone
who will give up
his own lovingness
in order to love
another being.

Chapter Thirty-two

The Flute Maker

I am the Flute but the music is Thine.
                                    Mevlana Jelaluddin Rumi

THIS IS THE STORY of a flute maker. Certain experiences arise in our lives to act as signposts along the Way. 'Look to the stars,' we are told. Look to the signs! This is a story about asking permission and living in the question. Like all real stories it can be understood on many levels.

Just outside of Taos in New Mexico there is a very old settlement called Taos Pueblo. It is a magical place and is unspoiled by the modern world. There is no electricity, no telephones, or television. People live as they have for over a thousand years.

Many years before, I had been privileged to meet an old man called Teles Good Morning, who was one of the Elders who lived there. When I moved to Santa Fe I went to see him once again, and he gave me a blessing, touching me with eagle wing feathers and praying in his own language. It was very moving. As I was leaving, I heard the sound of an Indian flute. There was nobody around actually playing the flute. I simply heard the sound in the wind. Then I suddenly remembered the very first time I had heard this sound. The sound was so very unique and almost haunting, and I remember making a vow to myself that one day I would find such a flute and learn how to play it. I had heard the Shakuhachi flute in Japan and the Ney in Konya, Turkey, but for some reason it was the Indian flute which sounded an echo in my own heart, more than any of the others.

As soon as we were settled in our house, in the hills above Santa Fe, I began a search for the right flute or, better still, the right flute maker. There is a famous Sufi story about a glassblower who fashions a glass cup to contain wine. At the end of the story, Mevlana says that we should not worry about the cup or even the wine, but immerse ourselves in the breath of the glassblower.

In Santa Fe there was a huge Indian Market going on in the town. It was a very popular annual event which went on for about a week. Indians come from all over the States and from Canada to meet, to have their gatherings and powwows, and to display and sell their incredibly beautiful pottery, jewellery, paintings and sculptures. We were told that over sixty thousand visitors were coming for that brief week. I thought, surely, I could find my Indian flute here at this market, but because it was so huge, it would be like looking for a needle in a haystack!

However, off I went searching through all the different exhibits and stalls, trying not to get too caught up in the beauty around me, also trying not to get caught up in the crowds that seemed to pour over the town plaza like a tidal wave. I saw silver and turquoise jewellery that shone brightly in the sun. I saw paintings that I wanted to hang on every wall of my house. I saw Navajo rugs that would add grace to any floor. There were wood carvings and stone sculptures, traditional religious carvings, and belts made of multi-coloured miniature beads. And with all the American Indians dressed up in their costumes, dancing and beating their drums, the whole picture was filled with colour, music and joyful greetings. But for some reason I could not find even one Indian flute. Drums yes, but flutes no! Not one single person sold traditional Indian flutes. It seemed almost incredible. I looked and I looked. There must be a flute!

Then, one day as I was walking away from the centre of the plaza, I caught sight of a man holding out a flute in his hands. He was handing it to the owner of one of the booths which sold Indian jewellery. For a moment I was trans-fixed, as I saw the flute change hands. Then the man who gave the flute walked towards me. I stopped him and asked him if he was a genuine flute maker. He nodded 'yes' to me, but then told me that he had just sold the last one. He went on to inform me that he always sold a flute to that particular man each year at the Indian Market.

My next question was the question I could not ask him. I wanted to know if he was really the flute maker that I was looking for. Did he know about The Breath? Perhaps he was just an ordinary flute maker. How was I to know? We talked for a long time. His Indian name was George Deer Tracks. Finally we arranged that he would indeed make me a flute. He lived nearly six hours away by car, so he agreed to bring it back to Santa Fe the next time he came. Two weeks later, I met him in the plaza early in the morning. I remember there was no one else around. The cleaners had been there, and the white benches were all wet from being washed. I bought the flute.

Still, I had no idea how to play it. I knew only that it

was a flute from the Lakota-Sioux tribe, and he had given me a piece of paper with some typed instructions as to how to tune it. The next morning I tentatively started to make some notes on it. It made a beautiful sound, and it looked very beautiful, as well as being very well crafted. But, it was not *the* flute! I don't know how I knew this, but I knew it. Nonetheless, in the next months I practised the art of flute-playing. Perhaps I had to first learn how to play an Indian flute, before I could realize how to recognize the breath of its maker from the sound of the wind passing through.

We can remember; the distant reaches of the past contain something of our own destiny. Then we may reach out for it. Perhaps we are a little afraid, and hold back, not wanting to put a foot in the wrong direction. Perhaps we do not yet know the difference between fate and Destiny. But there is the memory in our souls of our origin, just as there was the memory of the flute music which had rested in my heart from those days in Taos.

I went on practising and playing the flute every morning after my prayers. Sometimes I would play with the windows open, calling to the birds and the little desert animals with my music. I felt they could hear in some magical way. But where, oh where, was my true flute that surely must be waiting for me? Where would I find it? How would I start looking again? I did not give up the search. 'Perseverance furthers', as it says in the *I Ching*.

Whenever I went into town I would walk into each shop that might sell Indian flutes, or which might lead me to the next clue in my search through the maze. I met American Indians from many different tribes, and people in healing circles invited me to their ceremonies. I met many people, but politely declined their many invitations. I was on a search for just one thing – the flute maker!

Then one day I went into a pawnbroker's shop. I walked in, pretending to be interested in some of the articles for sale. One of the men in the shop was very smartly dressed, Spanish-American I believe, with a waxed mustachio and a belt flashing with silver Indian jewellery. He had on the usual ornate pointed boots. He didn't look surprised when I told him the Sufi story about the glassblower. Nor did he look surprised when I asked him if, by any chance, he knew of a flute maker who knew about The Breath. Picking up the telephone he dialled a number and spoke in Spanish to someone at the other end.

'Here,' he said, writing down an address on a piece of paper. 'Try there.' That was the end of the conversation.

When I went to this address, it turned out to be a store selling articles for interior design. Again I told my story to the owner. He listened but did not look up from his desk.

'I know the man you want,' he said. 'He is a Winnebago Indian, from up north in Wisconsin. He now lives near Albuquerque. Actually, he is coming here in a few days. There is to be a special ceremony, and he is to give the blessing in the Indian meeting hall.'

My heart started pounding. 'Can I see him?' I asked. 'I mean, would he make me a flute, do you think?'

The man went over to a table and picked up two flutes, which I had not seen when first looking around the store. 'He made these,' he said, holding out the flutes for me to hold. I looked at them. They were beautiful, but I knew that none of them was for me. There was something more in all this searching. I knew I had to meet the flute maker.

I did everything I could to go to the special ceremony,

but it was not meant to be. For some reason, I was not allowed to attend the ceremony. Perhaps it was only meant for the Indian people, who could truly understand the ceremonial rituals and the meaning of the sacred objects that are used. Many non-Indian people try to become Indians, but they can never be what they are not.

Still, I thought I might be able to find the flute maker at the shop where the owner had shown me the flutes. He did mention that the flute maker might, or might not, be in there that day at a certain tentative time, 'Indian time, you know,' said the owner. I arrived precisely at the time given to me, but there was no sign of the flute maker.

I told the owner, 'I will come back in one hour.' Then I made a visualization of the meeting and offered up a prayer. In exactly one hour I walked back in. Sitting on a stool was a man with dark black hair falling from underneath the hat on his head. He was perhaps fifty years old, or so, but it was hard to tell. Beside him on a chair sat his wife. We looked at each other, inquisitively.

'Ho,' he said. He must have known I was in search of him.

We shook hands and introduced ourselves. He told me his name in public was Roger, but said that I was not ready yet to hear his true Indian name. I told him the story of the glassblower. I told him some stories about healing and about my life, going on and on, one word falling into another.

'Sit down,' he said, 'You're making me nervous!'

I believe from that moment our friendship was sealed.

He went on, 'I might make you a flute. I could. But I'm not sure. I don't know you enough yet. And what do you want it for anyway?' he asked. He wanted to know about the quality of my intention.

We talked for a good hour. He asked me a lot of questions, and I answered them sincerely from my heart. But there was a surprising twist to the conversation. For I had actually intended to test him – to hear the sound of his voice – to discover if he knew about The Breath. Yet the man was actually testing me! Perhaps he was listening to the sound of my voice, and from where it came, to discover if *I* knew about The Breath.

'In our tradition,' he said, with his deep brown eyes cutting right through me, 'you have to be totally honest. I must know you. Then I will make a flute for you.'

He invited me to his house near Albuquerque. Two weeks later we drove there. When I was sitting in his small living room he asked, 'What is your animal?'

It was an unexpected question, which took me by surprise. I glanced at my wife, who looked as bewildered as me. 'My animal?' I quizzed back.

Roger said, 'Yes. What is your power animal?'

I remembered then that power animals are held with high regard in the Native American traditions and in the Way of the Shaman. These are guardians and guides from another world, and each kind of animal empowers one with certain unique qualities and abilities. According to some traditions, people on The Path have at least one major power animal, or animal guide, at any one time, to help them on the Journey.

'Well, to be honest,' I replied, 'I've never given this much thought. I don't know,' I replied, 'We don't have that sort of tradition, but please, if you wish, I give you permission to *see* my animal, if it will help you to make my flute . . .' He smiled and then I took my leave, promising to return in one week. The flute would be ready then, he said. On the long drive home, I could feel my heart pounding in the centre of my chest, which for me is always a sign that Destiny is most certainly at work.

One week later I went back to finally receive my flute. With both of his hands, Roger handed me the wooden Indian flute, as I received it with both my hands. I expressed to Roger my sincere gratefulness and appreciation for his work. Sweeping my hand along the smooth finish of the wood, I could feel the skill and love of the craftsman, the flute maker.

The flute felt right. I placed it up to my mouth and breathed out a note so fresh, so delicate, so peaceful. It was a sound of love. The one note seemed to carry right through the walls, round the world, then echoing back into the room. It lingered in the air long after the fullness of my breath. I knew this was my flute. And from the sound of my own breath passing through it, I knew for certain that the flute maker knew The Breath. Once again, I expressed my gratitude. Then I asked him what was my power animal.

'It's a bird. It's a Falcon,' he said, his great brown eyes smiling with such warmth.

One morning, some weeks later, as the sun rose up over the mountains, I touched a note on my flute that seemed to come from another world. It soared high into the air, reaching out and bringing down through my heart an answer to the inner prayer carried by the sound of the flute. I was suddenly aware of a strong presence just out-side the window in front of me. At the time, I was kneeling on my prayer rug and the window was wide open.

Suddenly, I heard a high-pitched cry from outside. I looked up and out towards the sun. There, sitting on a branch of our small pine tree was a peregrine falcon. He was just sitting there watching me. For a few minutes there was only silence, as the peregrine and I breathed together. Then he flew on and away over the valley. I never saw him again.

It is often in the silence that follows a storm that a sign is given, showing us that the Way has been found.

Chapter Thirty-three

THE BEAR AND THE RIVER

HOW CAN A STORY begin without a question? Perhaps our lives are only a repetition of memory patterns, thought-forms, and unnecessary suffering. Then, maybe a person comes into your life and asks a question which produces such a shock that it changes your whole pattern of living.

I know a man who came from a working-class family in Ireland. He left home when he was very young and travelled the world, as I have done. At one time, he was a logger in Borneo. He has done many things. Later in his life he became a leader of one of the more advanced spiritual centres in the world, located in the mountains of New Mexico. During the time he spent there, his wife developed cancer. I had the privilege of being part of the helping team of healers and now she has cancer no more – she looks after *other* people who have cancer.

He first heard me speak in California. At the end of the talk, I informed the audience that I was off to Vancouver the next morning to give a seminar. Something in my talk had touched him, because he ended up driving all the way to Canada to meet me. He and his friends took turns driving and arrived the next evening just in time for my talk. It's very unusual for an Irishman to drive one thousand miles to hear someone else talk. We became instant friends.

Years went by, the tides of life drifted back and forth. This friend started a bookshop in Santa Fe, New Mexico, which became very popular and well-known. When I moved to Santa Fe, he and I would meet occasionally. One day, he telephoned me to ask a question.

'Reshad,' he said, 'I once heard you speak about the inner meaning of the Virgin Mary, that after the time of the Virgin Mary there is no need to think. This changed something in me. But what does it actually mean?'

The question took me by surprise. I *did* know something about the Virgin Mary, in relation to the perfect Matrix of Life, yet, could I truly answer the deeper nature of his question which had come from his heart, and not just his head? I am not a religious scholar and I haven't read loads of books on these things. I wasn't raised a Catholic and I'm not a churchgoer. My knowledge is not so much of the outer form of religious ideas and beliefs, but an understanding of inner and hidden meanings, an understanding given to me from my own experiences, from my meditations, and from the many teachers who blessed my path.

The Virgin Mary is often seen as the archetypal Woman and Perfect Matrix of Life, having all of divine potential within Her, being the universal womb of all potential. I asked inside myself if I might be able to help him understand what I knew about this. I felt that we should take a walk together, somewhere in nature. I didn't know New Mexico very well yet, so I asked him to find a beautiful place to walk, near water because water, for me, is the symbol of flow and the feminine nature. Always remember that our bodies are made up of about eighty-five per cent water. My friend agreed to find a walk.

So a few days later he picked me up in his car and took me to the river Rio Grande. We stopped by a bridge and walked along the river for miles. During the walk, I remembered his question but did not speak directly about it. I just kept the question in my heart, as he must have shared the same question in his. Often, if we hold a question deep in our heart, the answer may appear anywhere and at any time, if we can just trust that we are given all the knowledge we may need.

I still did not know how I would answer his question, or how it might get answered, yet I remained in a state of allowing the answer to come, in its own time and in its own way. So we simply walked, enjoying the unique beauty all around us, and we talked together as friends.

After a long time walking, and feeling that we needed a rest, I saw a large beautiful tree near the riverside, which shaded a comfortable place to sit. So I said to myself, 'There I will give a discourse on the inner meaning of the Virgin Mary.' But at that precise moment, Hubert decided to take action.

And who is Hubert? Hubert is the nickname for my stomach. And Hubert has absolutely no interest in the spiritual path, whatsoever. Hubert expresses himself whenever and wherever. When Hubert needs to go and do his thing, I am obliged to follow. He always gets his way, sooner than not. Well, at this moment, Hubert was really growling, being very demanding. I had to do his bidding, fast!

I said to my friend, 'You go and sit down by that tree

over there. Get the tape recorder ready, and I'll be right back . . . nature calls!'

I quickly ventured out into the small forest of pines and scrub bushes just above us. As I was doing what I had to do, I had a very strange sense of a presence, very close to me. I did not know what it was because there were trees everywhere. Suddenly, I realized what it was: within about one metre from me, through the branches of this small scrub pine tree, I could see two eyes and a nose. It was a very large bear.

What would you do? Your trousers down, and then right in front of you there is a bear who could be dangerous! Do you finish off what you are doing or do you run? I did both. Having pulled up my trousers, I fled down towards the big tree, on the run, and my friend was sitting there with the tape recorder, waiting for me to give my talk about the Virgin Mary. Panting slightly I said, 'There is a bear!'

He said, 'No, there are no bears here.'

I said 'Look.' And I pointed out that, close to us, on the sand by the river, there were a bear's footprints. I said, 'Have you not seen? That is a bear's footprints.'

I was still doing up my belt and then I gave a discourse on the Virgin Mary. 'Ever since the *time* of the Virgin Mary, there is no need to think.' That is a great statement. How can we accept Jesus Christ without accepting the Virgin Mary? If we accept Mary we have no more need to think because the spirit of God resonates in our heart.

Does it take a bear and a tummy ache to listen?

Chapter Thirty-four

BLACK CROW

I CANNOT QUITE remember how young I was when I fell in love with the American Indians. Perhaps when I was very young, someone came to our house and talked about the Indians. Perhaps someone read stories to me. All I know is that something very real remains in my memory. It is not a glamorous image of Indians dressed in feathered war bonnets or fighting bloody battles. Rather, it is a memory of the sacredness of all Life, and of men and women working together with a common purpose. It is a memory of dignity and courage, of eagles flying high towards the sun, and the drumming and dancing – the endless drumming in the Dance of Life.

There is a beautiful church in Santa Fe, New Mexico. It is a *sanctuario* dedicated to Our Lady of Guadeloupe. It was here that I gave my first major talk in Santa Fe. The title was 'The Spiritual Warrior'. This is the sort of title which can open up all sorts of possibilities. I don't like to limit myself to talking on just one specific subject. I have a reputation of 'talking round and round in circles'. People may criticize me for this, and they may think that I haven't prepared the talk very well, but 'talking round in circles' without the prop of logical and sequential time is not so easy. I call it the 'scatter technique', like scattering wild flower seeds on to open land. A story here and there, with some commentary scattered around. There may be no apparent logic or ordered sequence to what I say, but some of the better listeners see the connection, or they see in these stories a reflection of their own experience.

However it's not my intention to confuse people. It's just that the Truth cannot always be told in a logical order or put into an organized system. Such attempts can actually cause problems later on. A great Sufi Master, Ibn al-'Arabi, said 'The Divine Guidance is to lead us to the point of perplexity.' The point of perplexity may be the only time we ask a real question.

On the night of this particular talk, it was freezing cold and pitch-black. There was no moon, and clouds veiled the stars. I walked to the church, muffled up against the wind that cut down the streets from the north. I thought about the evening to come. The few hundred people who were coming would arrive at the last minute. They would find their seats, and some would carefully choose the ones that were near the door. If they didn't like what I said they would slip out quietly. If, on the other hand, they were the sort of people who get angry, they would sit right at the end of the aisles by the wall. In that way, if they got up to leave they could cause a suitable disturbance and disrupt the energy in the room. I was used to all of this.

Before a talk, I always try to find some quiet little corner, where I can sit and centre myself in the breath. I become sensitive to the people seated and arriving, and I pray that I may be allowed to be of service. On that particular night I found a tiny chapel at the back of the church, where I could be private.

I was sitting quietly, and just before the time when I was meant to begin, I heard a knocking on the fire-exit door, close to where I was sitting. The knocking sounded urgent, so I went to see what was going on. I stopped at the door and wondered if it was wise to open it. After all, it could be anyone, and there are less than reputable characters in Santa Fe. On top of that, the custodian of the church had left for the evening, giving me his keys in case of an emergency. I stood in the relative warmth and safety of the church and wondered what to do. However, the knocking got louder and more insistent. Taking a step backwards as I opened the heavy door with its iron lock, I peered out into the dark. For a moment all I could see was pitch-black, but then as my eyes adjusted I saw a young American Indian standing there just outside the door. He was small, very dark-skinned, and his hair was tied back in a pony-tail wrapped around with coloured cloth. His eyes were as bright as early night stars. In one of his hands he held a piece of paper. The presence of this man was almost overwhelming.

'Is he here?' asked the man, holding out the paper towards me. 'I need to see him, please. Is he here?' he repeated.

At such moments it is difficult to get everything into focus. I was just about to go out and talk to two hundred people who might or might not be friendly. The man who was to introduce me had disappeared, and the caretaker was out for the evening. It was freezing cold and dark, and here was an Indian with a piece of paper. Nothing seemed to quite add up.

'Who, who do you want?' I spluttered.

'Is he in?' he asked again, this time more strongly.

'Well, no he isn't,' I replied, thinking he was talking about the caretaker. 'He's out for the evening I'm afraid, and he won't be back until later.'

'But I have to see him and give him this,' said the Indian once again.

Now I was definitely losing my presence of mind. I could hear that the introductory music had already stopped, signifying that it was time for me to start the lecture, and there was still no sign of my friend who was meant to be introducing the evening.

'Look,' I said, rather impatiently, 'I am just about to give a talk here in the church, and the caretaker is out, but I will finish my talk by quarter to ten, and then he'll be back and then you can give it to him yourself. Right?'

I started to close the door, but there was something so strange in the atmosphere that I really did not know what to say. Nor did I want to send the man away. He remained standing there without any visible sort of movement. He didn't smile and his eyes never left my own. It was all very odd. Time stood completely still as he, once more, pushed the piece of paper towards me.

'Look, I'm sorry,' I said, 'I really have to go, but please do come back at a quarter to ten.'

I closed the door very gently, but found myself shaking. At that moment my friend arrived.

'Where have you been?' he asked, rather upset. 'I've already introduced you, and they're all waiting for you.'

There was no time to explain. Gathering myself together, as best I could, I walked out in front of the audience and began my talk. Most of that evening remains a complete blank. I can only recollect seeing thirty or so people leave rather crossly after about fifteen minutes, pushing their way out and breathing with a grating sound as though they had swallowed dry and dusty sand. I had probably upset the images they had of what spiritual teachers should say, or perhaps I did not fit into their expectations. So very often, people only want others to agree with their accepted beliefs. They don't want to learn or to see life from another perspective. It would make them feel too uncomfortable and insecure.

I did finish my talk at precisely ten o'clock, just as I had visualized and agreed to. With correct visualization and agreement you don't really need a watch or a clock. After all, it is we who create time in our lives. I finished the night with a song, as I often do, about joy and freedom. Then I went back to the little chapel to sit alone and just breathe, to unwind and be grateful. Gratefulness is what counts in the long run.

After a while, I went back out to the main part of the church. The whole place was almost completely empty, though some people were standing around talking. I stood at the same spot where I had faced all the many people. Then a man appeared from the other end of the church. He was walking up the main aisle towards me. It was the same Indian man I had encountered at the fire-exit. And he was still holding the little piece of paper. He continued to walk intently towards me. My heart sank, as I realized that all along I had been the person he had come to see. Can you imagine how I felt?

It suddenly dawned on me that I had completely blown it. I stood there much taller than he, but felt so very small. He must have stood outside in the cold on that freezing night, waiting until the lecture was over, simply because I had not invited him in. The American Indians have certain manners. They do not force their personal business on others, and they do not come into a place unless invited. I had broken one of the most important rules of good conduct in any real tradition. I felt completely humiliated and totally devastated.

He walked right up to me, his eyes fixed on mine. He held out his little piece of paper. Looking at him, I saw no sign of anger or resentment.

'My name is Black Crow,' he said, 'They say that you sing to people, and that they sometimes get better. Our medicine has not worked. Will you please sing for this person?'

Once again, he thrust the little piece of paper towards me. This time I took it. I took it in my right hand. Suddenly the tension broke between us. Something moved deeply within him, I could see it in his eyes. An overwhelming love for this man filled up inside me. I wanted so much that he forgive my stupidity.

He simply nodded to me a silent thank-you, then turned around and slowly walked away down the aisle. By now, I was nearly in tears, a mixture of shame and gratefulness. Shame that I had been so insensitive and unaware in a moment of need, and grateful for having been allowed to meet this dignified American Indian.

What I learned from his hand-written letter was that he had read an article in a local Santa Fe newspaper, a story about a brave young woman who had conquered a very serious case of cancer. I had been mentioned in the article as one of the people instrumental in helping her to recover. I had heard of her illness from mutual friends when I was in Europe, and knowing that sound and song are better than a lot of talk, I picked up the telephone and sang a song to her from my heart. It was the Christian Prayer of Abandonment:

> *Father*
> *into Thy hands I abandon myself*
> *Do with me whatever You will*
> *and whatever You do*
> *I will thank You*
> *and remain ever grateful*
> *Let Thy Will be done in me*
> *as in all Your creatures*
> *Father into Thy hands I commit my spirit*
> *I give it to You*
> *with all the love in my heart,*
> *For I love You, Lord,*
> *and so long to give myself,*
> *with a trust*
> *beyond all measure.*

Black Crow had heard that I would be at this church in Santa Fe on this particular date. He had come a long way to meet me from the mountains where he lived. Yet he could not have realized that I was the one he was looking for. I never saw him again.

The next morning I dialled the number that he had written down on the little piece of paper that he had brought to the *sanctuario*. I was not sure what to expect, and when Black Crow had said that their 'Medicine' had not worked, it was difficult enough to imagine that I could personally be of help. The Native Indians use the word 'Medicine' in such a way that it carries many different meanings. In this case I was convinced that they had used their own methods of healing, but that the person I was meant to telephone had not responded to their old, traditional ways.

All I had was the telephone number. I did not at first realize that it was the number of Black Crow's wife, nor did I know that she was suffering from a serious illness.

A man answered the phone. I tried to explain to him what had happened the night before, but he did not understand, and he even sounded a little angry. I asked him very quietly who he was and I was informed that he was the father of the woman who was ill. It also took very little time to realize that he was a white man and that he did not approve of mixed marriages in any way. He did not allow her to come to the phone, but told me in no uncertain terms to mind my own business.

So I never did get a chance to sing to her a song from my heart. But then, nothing happens unless the time is right in this world. As the old saying goes, 'Don't push the river.' I had done all I could to make contact, but surely there are so many invisible and intangible factors involved in these matters. And God knows best!

Chapter Thirty-five

NATIVE WISDOM

I BEGAN GIVING regular classes in Santa Fe, and one series of discourses was on the nature of time. Most people think that time only goes from A to Z, rather than understanding that time goes both ways. We can easily understand that time is going out, or running out, from the moment we are born to the moment we die to this world. But we forget that time is coming in, as well, as we make space for time.

We usually regard time as ticking away, as we run after time, trying to keep up with it. Time appears to pass by, and we appear to be victims of time. We can let it run us over, or we can consciously work with time, through intention, visualization, agreement and knowledge. Time has many dimensions, and there are different aspects to each dimension. The complete nature of time is difficult to understand, because one really has to experience what it is like to be both *in* time and *outside* time – at the same time.

There is a saying that 'Some people see God in creation and some people see creation in God, yet the Sufi is one who sees both at once.' To experience the different dimensions of time, simultaneously, it is necessary to live life passionately and 'to love very, very much', as a close friend of mine, Gurdjieff's niece, Luba once said.

The day after giving one of these seminars on time, I went out for a walk on the streets of Santa Fe. I have always loved walking. I let the wind blow me from place to place, until I end up in a learning experience. If I go with my heart and my hands open, something always happens. Then, I take home whatever I've learned, distil it, then pass it on to others.

At this particular time, I happened to walk into a shop selling Native American crafts and jewellery. I had been in the shop once before, looking for the flute maker. Here I had met the owner, an extraordinary Native American woman called Coming Morning. But because I had been on such an intense quest for my flute, I hadn't really given much time to looking around the shop. Nor had I really got to know Coming Morning. I had a strong intuition that she knew some of the mystical wisdom of the Native Indian tradition. Now, it was my intention to ask her a question, and to open my mind and heart in order to receive the answer.

When I walked into the shop, Coming Morning was busy serving customers. I realized I would have to wait in order to speak with her. I might even have to wait a long time. I wondered, how much time did I really have? But if there was ever going to be a time to really meet, it could very well be this day. The people who were there finally left, having bought some beautiful pieces of jewellery.

I had been walking around the shop. The front part was really a gallery of exquisite museum pieces made by the

Plains Indians. The quality was breathtaking. There were Indian shields, sacred artefacts, paintings and other works of art made by contemporary Native American artists. There was beadwork with colours bursting out, like spring moving into summer.

I looked at Coming Morning. She stood at a corner of the room in an aura of perfect silence and peace, with a very definite sense of pride and dignity. This time I caught her eye. She greeted me with a simple smile and a silent nod of respect, but said nothing. I nodded back to her. I was happy that she had recognized me. But out of respect, I decided to wait for her to initiate any spoken conversation. I decided to remain silent until invited to speak.

The shop was truly remarkable, and I revelled in the spirit of all this beauty and excellent craftsmanship. Coming Morning still remained silent. I believe she knew that I wished to speak with her, but she purposefully remained distant.

Finally I broke the silence and commented on the shop's special quality of beauty. I asked her if she remembered me from some months before, as I was looking for a flute. She remembered. I spoke to her of my passionate appreciation for the Native Americans and we shared with each other how we both happened to be in Santa Fe. In almost no time at all we became friends. She said to me,

'I can tell that you are a white man who can listen and hear. That is very rare indeed. So perhaps I can share some native wisdom. I think that's what you really came here for, isn't it?'

'Well,' I said, 'I would like to learn more about the native wisdom. I would like to learn more about our sacred connection with the earth. In my tradition this world is a reflection of the higher worlds. They say that God created the world in order to see Himself.'

She invited me into her office at the back of the shop, offered me a chair and sat down, looking at me with gentle eyes that seemed to be filled with compassion. She said, 'But many of you have forgotten the drum.'

There was a long pause, as Coming Morning studied my reaction. What did she mean? An image came into my mind of a medium-sized Indian drum decorated with coloured feathers and animal designs. I love music and I used to have some bongo drums during the sixties. But I hadn't played a drum in many years. Coming Morning continued,

'You have all your spiritual practices, you meditate, and you do all sorts of fascinating things, but you forget the heartbeat of the Earth. That is why we use the drum – to remember the heartbeat of the Earth.'

Again, she paused and studied me, waiting in a state of absolute patience, as her words and meaning sank into me. I knew she was a true teacher because of her ability to awaken something in me. I wanted to understand. I re-membered the earth below my feet. I began to feel the heart-beat of the earth. She continued,

'Put the drum into your life. Then you will remember that we are all custodians of this planet. You need to make some time to feel the earth. Put your ear to the ground and listen to the heartbeat of the Mother. Let your own heartbeat resonate with the heartbeat of Earth. Then perhaps you will begin to understand the real meaning of time.'

How uncanny that she should mention 'time'! I could follow what she was saying, and I knew she was speaking the truth. It seemed so coincidental to think that I had just been giving classes about time! I contemplated on the connection between the drum, the heartbeat and time. She said,

'Your people do not understand time as we do. You get anxious when we don't work on the same sort of time as you do.'

I thought about how people often make fun of 'Indian time'. How in our modern world we rush about, always looking at our watches. Always trying to fill up our time with busy schedules or various entertainments, but never experiencing the inner space of time and never simply being present right here in the moment. 'Indian time' is following a natural rhythm of time and only doing things when the time is just right. She continued,

'Perhaps if I tell you a story from our tradition, it will help you to understand this better. I will tell you about the gourd, or what is called the rattle. If you come to our powwows you will see and hear the rattle working together with the music, the dance and the drum. They all work together, like a family. The drum, the rattle, the singing and the dance . . . it is all part of our tradition. We make our instruments from what the Earth provides. These instruments can also be used as "medicine tools".

Our healers often use the drum and the gourd, as well as song and prayer.'

I nodded my agreement. She continued,

'To know the full meaning of the gourd you must make one. First of all, you must find a gourd. The gourd comes from something that we grow, then dry in the sun over a period of time. But the gourd itself makes no sound. You have to find something very special to put into the gourd, before you seal it with the handle that is used to shake the gourd.

'In our tradition, a young man is sent on a vision quest by his teacher or Elder. He is sent out alone to a mountain for three days and three nights without food or water, in order to be given his vision by Wakan' tanka, which is our name for the Divine, the Great Spirit. When he comes back, he goes to his teacher and describes his visions. Then, the teacher, or Elder, helps him to understand the meaning of these visions and he points him in the right direction for the future of his life. He may suggest what sort of work would be best for the young man, suggesting what sort of function could be fulfilled for the community and for the earth as a whole. Then, if it is right, they will send him out to search the land for an ant-hill. There are many big ant-hills out there in the desert. He is told to go find an ant-hill, because ants know the secret of time.'

Again, she brought up the nature of time. I listened even more carefully. She said,

'The ants know the secret of time because they were

here before us. That is what is said in our tradition. There-fore, to understand time, we go to the ants. The young man finds an ant-hill and discovers that ants collect little pebbles and gems from the soil. He is instructed to collect seventy-two of these pebbles, without disturbing the ants or their home. He must also ask permission from Wakan' tanka to remove any pebble. It takes as long as it takes to find and collect seventy-two pebbles. The young man must be very patient. He must be careful as well, for these ants can bite! The whole task might even take years, because he may only be able to collect just a few pebbles from any one ant-hill before needing to find another one. When he has finally collected seventy-two of these pebbles, he returns to the Elder. He is then instructed to find a gourd and make a hole in the top of the gourd, and then he drops the little pebbles into the gourd. It is then sealed with a short wooden stick of just the right thickness, which becomes the handle of the rattling gourd. The task is then completed. The gourd may be painted with special colours and symbols. It may be decorated with natural things of the earth. Then, the gourd may be taken to the Dance, to the sacred ceremonies, or possibly be used for healing.'

All of this was very fascinating and helpful to my under-standing of the Indian Way, but I wondered why the num-ber seventy-two? Seven and two add up to nine, which is the number of completion in the Sufi tradition. Also, it was said by the Prophet Mohammed, 'Take seventy-two to the mountain', because at that time there were seventy-two tribes which he united into one Whole.

Coming Morning went on to say that the meaning of the rattle, or the gourd, was that Sound had brought all of us together. Seventy-two different aspects of life, or ways of looking at life, or different kinds of people, all come together in one sacred object, representing the Mother Earth. All make sound together, a beautiful sound of harmony and rhythm.

'So,' she said, 'maybe now you'll understand more about time, Indian time. Just remember the drum and remember the gourd. Remember the rhythm and the Dance. Let the beat of your drum rhythm be in harmony with the heartbeat of Mother Earth, in passion and in love. Let the gourd be filled with all the divine aspects of Life. Let the many come together to make the Sound of Unity.'

She looked at me deeply and seriously, but through her eyes she smiled. I could sense her own love and passion for life. 'Thank you for listening,' she said, 'I feel that you understand. Now you should go. I must get back to my work. There will be another time.' She winked at me.

Just then, the shop door opened and a couple walked in. Together we walked out of her little office, and Coming Morning went on to serve her customers.

During the next few months I would often walk into her shop to see if we could talk again. Sometimes the shop would be empty, which allowed something very profound to happen between us. Other times there would be a stream of people coming in, so we wouldn't be able to have a deeper connection. When there were other people in the store, she would always serve these people first, out of respect. I knew that if we were ever going to communicate from the heart, I would have to wait for her and she would wait for me. I would wait, and she would wait, and we would wait. She was always very patient with everyone. Occasionally, even if the shop was empty, she just didn't seem to want to talk. It wasn't the right time.

One day, when I had waited to see if it was the right time, she really had me wondering if I had enough patience to even be in the same room with her. There was a group of people browsing through the store. They were asking her silly questions, but she remained very patient.

Suddenly, she walked away from everyone and came straight towards me. She whispered in my ear, 'Reshad, who is going to wake them up?'

Chapter Thirty-six

THE ABALONE SHELL

I WAS INVITED to San Francisco to give a talk and an interview on radio. In the early morning of the interview, I drove up the coast road toward the city. As I drove up the winding road I remembered a certain hidden beach which I had often visited with my wife, and which I had mentioned in my book *Breathing Alive*.

We had discovered this hidden beach one day while exploring the coast. On this beach you could always find at least one red abalone shell that had washed up onto the sand. But it was not necessarily easy. For unless we were very awake, we wouldn't notice them, even in the light of the sun. We could only find them when we were in a heightened state of awareness.

I decided to stop there and look for one of these beautiful abalone shells for my friend, Coming Morning. I knew she would treasure it, as in the Native American tradition, shells are considered valuable and sacred. They frequently burn sage and sweetgrass in them. Although I searched carefully I could not find a single abalone shell on the beach. Perhaps too many people discovered the beach after my book was published so that there were no abalone shells left.

I drove on to the radio station empty-handed. The interviewer for the programme was a woman whom I'd known for some years. She was a natural listener. After the two-hour programme, at the end of the evening, I returned to my motel to have a rest.

The next morning, the manager of the motel knocked on my door saying, 'I have a parcel for you.' I took the package and opened it. I couldn't believe what I found – it was the most perfect red abalone shell that I'd ever seen. The gift was from my friend at the radio station. I was truly amazed, for I'd told her nothing about my search to find the shell for Coming Morning. I telephoned the station right away to thank her for this extraordinary gift and to share the joy I felt in receiving it.

Later in the day, I flew back to Santa Fe. I wrapped the abalone shell in beautiful paper and went to see Coming Morning. I was excited to bring her a gift that I felt she and her clan would like for their ceremonies. However, things didn't work out as I thought they would. I walked into the shop and presented the gift to her. Much to my surprise, she didn't even open it! I found out afterwards that this is normal behaviour for Native Americans. They always seem to disappear with their gifts and only rarely do they open them in front of people.

Two or three days later, I went back to see her. I was expecting a big 'thank-you' for giving her the shell. At first, she didn't look at me. She just bowed her head.

I was getting more and more uncomfortable when she finally looked up and said rather strongly, 'Why do you white people always want to find out whether we *like* your gifts, or not? Don't you know that all gifts come from the Great Spirit and all gifts finally return to Him?'

Chapter Thirty-seven

THE PIPE

ONE DAY I received a telephone call from Coming Morning. This was surprising because she seldom initiated communication. She seldom called on me. She said, 'Reshad, I have permission from my Elders to initiate you as a "Pipe Carrier".'

This surprised me even more. I wondered what was the meaning of all this. I knew this was a special honour, but should I accept it? I have found over the years that many groups have asked to initiate me into something or another, but I often declined because I knew it wasn't right. This time was different. I had come to respect Coming Morning and I appreciated the Native American way, and so we agreed on a date for the ceremony.

Then she said, 'I want you to find fourteen people with whom I can feel comfortable.'

What did she mean by that, I wondered? We cannot simply presume that others mean what we think they mean. Languages are different, cultures are different, and people are different. We need to respect these differences and learn to understand them. For me, respect precedes love. The word 'respect' originally comes from the Latin *respectare* which means 'to see again'. In the precise moment that we are free of our resentment, envy and pride, we are indeed the eyes through which God sees. From this clear seeing comes love, and love is the movement of beauty.

I knew many people in the area of Santa Fe, yet it wasn't very easy to find the right fourteen people. Eventually I found them. The special ceremony was to take place out in the open air and luckily we had an acre of land and a beautiful private garden in which to meet.

Coming Morning arrived with her son at the agreed time. She brought the same sacred robes I'd seen her wear at a private ceremony which she'd invited me to once before. Coming Morning had insisted that everyone present for the ceremony first prepare themselves by washing. In the Native American traditions purification is always the first step in any real ceremony or healing work.

I asked my wife to look after her, and she was taken to the bathroom to properly wash and change her clothes. My wife watched as Coming Morning very conscientiously washed her face, her arms and hands, and also her feet. In the Sufi tradition we wash ourselves in a certain way, in order to be perfectly clear and pure for the Presence of God, especially before prayers or ceremonies. My wife later told me that the two different traditions of washing were almost exactly the same. People often forget that right preparation and clear intention sets a pattern for what may come.

When we were all finally prepared, Coming Morning walked out into the night in full robes. She was so proud, and yet so humble. Actually, there was just the dignity that comes with carrying an unbroken line of sacred tradition.

We all assembled in the garden and formed a circle. Her son was sitting with a drum. He faced towards the east, while Coming Morning faced towards the west. My friends and I stood in silence, somewhat shy and not knowing what to do, though wanting to behave with the proper manners.

Coming Morning opened a pouch and brought out some herbs and sacred tobacco, and she handed some to each person. She also gave us pieces of white cloth and instructed us to each make a 'bundle' with the dried leaves. This, she told us, will be part of a ritual to help us let go of our own pain and also our pride. Her son began to drum. Then Coming Morning began to lead us in a very simple chant using certain sounds, again, similar to the Sufi Tradition. I thought how wonderful it was that my friends and students could witness and experience this essential similarity between two sacred traditions. Perhaps this was one of the reasons for all of us meeting together?

We had already built a sacred fire, as instructed, and now we were invited to take our bundles, one by one, to the fire. She asked us to put them close to the fire, rather than in the fire. Then we each returned back to the circle.

Coming Morning then brought out the sacred pipe and asked me to come forward to her. She had her back to the east and her son was now on my left beating the drum. I could sense that the people in the circle were deeply moved by what was happening. She said some words of prayer and offered up the pipe to Great Spirit. Then with both her hands she held out the pipe to me, and I received it with both my hands. Our eyes were locked together and we breathed as one. I glanced down at the pipe as I received it. Then my eyes returned again to Coming Morning, who now appeared to radiate a blue light.

While I held the sacred pipe to my heart, the whole sky suddenly lit up in front of me. I'm not exaggerating – I saw a vision of the resurrected Christ! He came to me as an Indian, with radiant lines of energy bursting forth from His Head. I then understood the meaning of the feathered headdresses worn by the old tribal Chiefs, which clearly show the burst of light that comes from the head when the Divine Presence is awakened. The experience was completely overwhelming. I stood there in the night air for what seemed to be an eternity. This vision will stay with me forever, but perhaps, it was already complete in my heart before it finally came to pass in the outer world. I felt absolutely humbled by the whole experience, and I was rendered speechless.

After the ceremony, we all returned to the house. We washed again, then sat down for some tea. When it was time for Coming Morning and her son to leave, I walked them out into the night. I asked Coming Morning, 'When do I smoke the pipe?' She looked at me and smiled. She said, 'Only when you are totally in despair or when completely in praise of the Great Spirit.'

She watched me to see if I understood. She went on to explain that the Sacred Pipe was originally given as a kind of tool for the two-legged ones to communicate with Great Spirit. 'With the Pipe, we send our prayers and our thanks to Great Spirit.' As one's prayer is held in the heart, the sacred tobacco is burned in the pipe, and one watches the prayer in the smoke rise up to Great Spirit. The sacred tobacco represents 'all our relations', all lives on earth, past, present and future. The rising smoke of their burned essence is like our own essence returning to Great Spirit from the fire of our own sacrifice or death of the ego. She went on to explain that some of the great Medicine Men and Women say that they work to become a clean pipe for Great Spirit to pass through. They offer themselves, as a clean pipe, to be of service here on earth to the Work and Breath of Great Spirit.

'So my friend,' she said, 'make good use of the Sacred Pipe, and always use it in deep respect.'

Her son then added, looking me straight in the eyes with tremendous honesty, 'Please remember what you have been given. And never forget the dignity of our People.'

'I never will,' I replied.

Coming Morning then added, 'Being a Pipe Carrier is a great honour in our tradition. It is not just meant for you. It is meant for a greater purpose. It is usually shared with others, in group prayer. So whenever you smoke the Pipe, you must remember All Our Relations and the Unity of All Life. Never forget to hold All of creation in your mind and heart.'

I still have the pipe to this day . . .

Chapter Thirty-eight

THE PORT

Walking along the port
quay-side
the tide
changing,
sails
flapping,
ropes pulling
to move
her
with the wind
and the tide.
I walk
the quay-side.

In front
a dog barks
chasing gulls.
They rise
on the thermals,
calling, calling
moving out
to the sea.

A couple
arm in arm
turn
as the boats
move out.

Below me
a fishing boat.
They are mending
the nets.
It is too early –
the tide must go
still further.
The sea bass
will be
by the reef.

Gulls rejoicing,
waiting, waiting.
The fishermen
will
return.

A feast
for white-plumed
sea birds.
The heads,
the pieces
left over.

And I
watch
the changing
of
the tide.

Chapter Thirty-nine

GOING HOME

SO OFTEN we make the best of plans, only for them to disappear into the mist. Perhaps we even have to start again just when we were convinced that the Way had been found. Our world can be shattered right in front of us, and it is surely only through patience and perseverance that we can proceed once more in our search for a true Reality. It can be said that we are guided, moved along the tracks of time in our search, and whatever is necessary is given to us and whatever is not needed for the good of the whole is finally taken away.

Through deep intuition we can be informed when a cycle is over. And so it was with my time in the United States. After much waiting, day after day, week after week, month after month, I finally received an invitation to go to Switzerland. I packed everything up and eventually came back to Europe.

There was one further thing to do. I had not seen the man who had been my teacher for many years. I wanted to go and pay my respects to him once more and to thank him. Although it had been necessary for us to be separated in this world of appearances, in the spiritual and invisible worlds there had been no distance between us. There had just been certain sacrifices that were necessary on the road I had chosen to travel.

When I arrived at his home, he was busy working on a translation of some sacred texts. Finally he appeared in the room and his eyes met mine with a look so deep and penetrating that is almost impossible to describe. The journey since I had left England flashed before me in one moment, in which I saw there had never been any separation. It had not been easy to be thrust out into a kind of wilderness armed only with a letter containing instructions to do my best to 'lead others to the knowledge which inevitably leads to love', as he had so often said.

It was also true to say that, at that time, things had been difficult between us. But this happens so often in teacher–pupil relationships, almost as though by some design, to prevent the pupil from identifying too much with the person who has been his guide on the Road. . . .

He smiled. We hardly spoke a word. There was nothing left to say. It was like crossing a bridge that had been set up at the beginning of time.

It was not long after my visit that I heard he had passed away.

Epilogue

Turning here on earth is turning to God. Turning is what we have been given by God to bring to this earth.

Once, when I was living in England my car had broken down by the side of the road. I saw a woman walking along the same road. Where was she going? Compassion is action without judgement. So I took action.

I called out to her, 'What are you doing here on this road?' And I didn't tell her that possibly this was the Road of Truth.

I was sitting on the side of the road and she came and sat down next to me. I asked her where she wanted to go. For a moment or two she couldn't even reply. Then she told me she had been raped and badly hurt.

We shared the silence for a while before I asked her one more time, 'Where do you want to go?'

She said, 'I just want to go home.'